IMAGES
of America

THE UNIVERSITY OF
PENNSYLVANIA BAND

IMAGES
of America

THE UNIVERSITY OF PENNSYLVANIA BAND

The University of Pennsylvania
Band Archives

ARCADIA
PUBLISHING

Published by Arcadia Publishing
Charleston SC, Chicago IL, Portsmouth NH, San Francisco CA

Library of Congress Catalog Card Number: 2006924868

For all general information contact Arcadia Publishing at: Telephone
843-853-2070
Fax 843-853-0044
E-mail sales@arcadiapublishing.com
For customer service and orders:
Toll-Free 1-888-313-2665

Visit us on the Internet at www.arcadiapublishing.com

*This "Highball Toast" goes to all members past, present, and future.
A Highball Toast also goes out to Christopher Mario (class of 1985)
and Walter Gallagher (class of 1937). Their generous gifts to our
organization have ensured another 100 years of vivid images,
stories of glory, and songs for our beloved alma mater,
the University of Pennsylvania.*

CONTENTS

ACKNOWLEDGMENTS

Countless Penn undergraduate members of the University of Pennsylvania Band have come and gone over the past 109 years, volunteering an incalculable number of hours to serve their alma mater. It is their collective commitment and accomplishments that we celebrate here.

The University of Pennsylvania Archives curates a vast historical collection. We are grateful for permission to publish many of the images presented that originate from their collection, as well as for the expert assistance of Mark Frazier Lloyd, director of archives, and Nancy R. Miller, public services archivist.

We wish to thank Erin L. Vosgien, senior editor at Arcadia Publishing, for her expert guidance and support during the writing process. We also thank Mary DiStanislao, Ed.D. (department of athletics); Ty Furman, M.F.A. (student performing arts); and Fran Walker, Ph.D. (division for the vice provost for undergraduate life) for their support of our organization and their guidance. Special thanks are also due to Bruce Montgomery, D.F.A., whose critical review and kind foreword helped mold the final product.

A committee of undergraduates and alumni was integral to the creation of this book, aiding through their research, writing, and enthusiasm. Credit for this final product is attributed to the following persons: Kushol Gupta, Ph.D. (class of 1997, assistant director); Christopher Przybyszewski (class of 1998); Pamela Rist (class of 2007); Melanie Foreman (class of 2008); Kirsten Blessing (class of 2006); Jessica Neiterman (class of 2006); Rebecca Goldman (class of 2008); Laura Vago (class of 2004); Greer Cheeseman (class of 1977, director); and Adam Sherr, M.S.Ed. (class of 1990, assistant director).

Lastly I wish to thank my wife and children for their support during this project: their unconditional support and love never go unappreciated or unnoticed.

—Kushol Gupta, Ph.D.

FOREWORD

It is a daunting task to be invited to write a foreword for a book about the history of the University of Pennsylvania Band. This book is so wonderfully complete in its coverage of the Penn Band and its unique place in the life of the university and contains such a rich treasure-trove of photographs and other illustrations, that anything I might add seems almost superfluous. On the other hand, I am so pleased at being asked to be a part of this happy enterprise that I accepted the responsibility at once.

Only a few student activities have so marvelously represented Penn throughout the country and—from its recordings, telecasts, and alumni loyalty—throughout the world as the University of Pennsylvania Band. One of the longest continuing traditions of my childhood was that Thanksgiving dinner never was permitted to begin until after the Penn–Cornell football game. Even though my father was a Princeton graduate, we would bundle up and join Penn's student body and alumni (and much of Philadelphia) in this annual ritual. We would loudly echo the students in their rousing chant "Fight like hell! Beat Cornell! No school Monday!" I am very sure the games always were great fun and sources of considerable spirit but, to me, the high point of the event was the lining up of the band in their long, dark-blue overcoats and visored caps, trumpets blaring the familiar fanfare notes of Tchaikovsky's 1812 *Overture*, and then marching off down Franklin Field from the east-end wooden goalpost in their astonishing trademark quickstep. It was a thrilling tradition to an impressionable young boy. And, while it is not exactly the same exercise today, I still get a delighted gut-reaction when the band enters the stadium so many years later. Memories fall hard. And thank goodness!

It was my very good fortune to have been one of the directors of this marvelous ensemble in the late 1950s and 1960s, and that is a fact of which I am extremely proud. I have been known to quip that I was "the worst band director ever to walk on Franklin Field." Actually that is not entirely true. But I was, indeed, privileged to be a part of the grand tradition and to have worked so closely with so many talented students. When I conduct the pit orchestras for the yearly Penn Singers' Gilbert and Sullivan productions, I know that I can call upon some members of the band for expert help. And the same was true over so many years when I conducted the Penn Glee Club's pit band. It is very gratifying to know that talented young men and women will share the musical expertise and spirit that has been so indelibly instilled in them by their joyous band participation.

It is equally wonderful to see evidences of all this talent and tradition now brought beautifully under the cover of a new interesting, delightful, and highly readable book. It will prove a treasured keepsake for the legions of men and women who already have been in the Penn Band and a marvelous eye-opener to the present and future students who are lucky enough to participate in it. It also should become a valuable reference for anyone interested in an important facet of University of Pennsylvania history and life.

—Bruce Montgomery, D.F.A.

INTRODUCTION

A renaissance in campus life occurred at higher institutions of learning across the United States in the late 19th century. This change was marked by a transition from the commuter-based "colonial colleges," built on religious affiliations, to secular institutions where a more cosmopolitan student body could reside. This conversion was marked by the development of professional schools, large-scale investment in new architecture, and a shift toward the German model of the modern research university. At the University of Pennsylvania, this change coincided with the university's move from Old City Philadelphia (the second move in its history) to the area immediately west of the Schuylkill River in 1872. A vibrant student community formed in West Philadelphia, one that engaged in intercollegiate sports, drama, and music as an escape from the rigors of academics. One of the activities born out of this sequence of events was the student marching band.

Marching band is an activity deeply rooted in military tradition, dating back to the 16th-century Ottoman Empire. As its importance to troop movement diminished, the military band evolved to become a ceremonial tradition of performance. By the mid-1800s, John Philip Sousa and other renowned American bandmasters successfully transferred the activity to popular mainstream culture. They inspired the country's interest in marching-band music with performances of their own popular compositions by ensembles of great renown. The earliest college marching bands appeared at the Big 10 schools in the Midwest during the 1870s and 1880s. Each was strongly influenced by the military band appearing earlier at West Point and the growing popularity of the activity. However, it was not until the late 1880s that marching bands began to appear at intercollegiate football games, with one of the earliest reported appearances occurring in 1887 at the University of Notre Dame.

Many aspects of the University of Pennsylvania Band (commonly called the Penn Band) have remained constant through its history. Since its inception in 1897, the band has been a fixture at athletic contests and annual campus rituals. It has served as the university's most audible ambassador to the local community and has provided the pomp and circumstance for formal celebrations and events. Above all else, it has been an outlet for undergraduates to practice their craft and enjoy their college experience outside the context of the classroom. The band has always been a primarily student-led group and has never been affiliated with any of Penn's academic departments. Its membership has been composed of true amateurs, performing not for scholarships or academic credits, but for their love of music and their alma mater. These guiding principles are embodied by the organization today and distinguish it from many university bands nationwide. These attributes are more remarkable in light of the fact that the organization is one of the most active in the United States. The band has performed with extreme regularity—anywhere from 60 to over 100 times in a given academic year.

However, not all things have remained constant for this student organization. In what is perhaps an oxymoron in the truest sense of the word, the Penn Band was once self-described in a late-1960s band recruiting brochure as "one of Penn's most progressive student traditions." This label is appropriate as illustrated by the inclusion of females and African Americans in its membership in the middle of the 20th century, as well as its departure from the traditional marching band uniforms and the abandonment of marching drill in favor of satire-based football halftime shows. One could argue that the Penn Band's willingness to adapt and change has enabled it to survive to today and thrive, whereas other, less-flexible student traditions (such as the pants fight and the Push Ball) and practices on the Penn campus have gone extinct.

Marching bands can be categorized according to their style and context of performance. In itself, the account of a military-style marching band might be described as commonplace. What sets apart the past of the Penn Band (and other Ivy-League bands) is its evolution from a military-style marching band into the Ivy-league style "scramble" band of the late 20th century. The collegiate scramble band (also know as "scatter band" or "Ivy-League-style band") is a distinct variety of performance ensemble. Scrambling is currently practiced by undergraduates around the country, including those at most of the Ivy-League schools, Rice University, and Stanford University. This brand of performance is characterized by football halftime shows built on wit and satire, where a comedic script is read over a stadium loudspeaker, and punch lines are delivered via the music selection and the formations made on the field.

The development of this style of performance was a gradual one, originating at Harvard and Columbia in the 1960s. The humorous halftime shows originally blended with traditional marching-band practices. It was not until the 1970s that a full abandonment of the traditional uniform and *espirit de corps* associated with the military style of performance was complete. This new form of marching-band performance is the style of choice for numerous programs among the highest echelons of academia.

Three student groups on Penn's campus stand out with regards to performance history: the Penn Band, the Penn Glee Club, and the Mask and Wig Club. All three organizations have remarkable records of achievement that date back to the late 19th century. What sharply contrasts the Penn Band from the other two organizations is its *modus operandi*: on rare occasion has the Penn Band been the primary focus of the occasion at which it performs, whether at an athletic contest or campus celebration. All three organizations have embraced considerable changes over their respective histories, whether it be in appearance, coed membership, or practice. Of the three groups, it could be argued that the Penn Band has undergone the most dramatic changes over the past 100 years.

This book celebrates the Penn Band and its proud tradition in pictures, tracing its colorful transformation, from its start as the prototype for modern collegiate marching bands, through times of war and social inequality, to its rebirth as the comedic Ivy-League-style scramble band. Underscored in this book are not only the aspects of the group that have remained the same over the past 100 years, but also the changes the band has undergone.

One

THE BIRTH OF THE UNIVERSITY OF PENNSYLVANIA BAND

"Shut up, Fresh!"

That was one of many jeers directed by residents of the Quadrangle (the primary student dormitory at the university at the time) toward freshman A. Felix DuPont (class of 1901), in response to his cornet performance one autumn afternoon in 1897. Shortly after that performance, DuPont was approached by classmate John Ammon (class of 1901) and others about forming a student band. Together they gathered the first 27 members of what would become the University of Pennsylvania Band.

This volunteer group was in immediate demand. In its first year, the band performed at student rallies and parades, at the new student union (Houston Hall), and twice for Pres. William McKinley. Concurrent with the birth of the fledgling band was the rise of college football. The university played its first intercollegiate football game against now-archrival Princeton University in 1876. Historic Franklin Field at the University of Pennsylvania was built in 1895, and by 1915, it was well-established that the "varsity" band would play at all football games and other occasions. It was seldom in these early years that the organization would encounter other collegiate bands at athletic contests; in this regard, the University of Pennsylvania was a pioneer.

In its first decades, the group boasted an annual membership that ranged from 25 to 40 members. After the signing of the armistice that ended World War I, college campuses across the country renewed their focus on academics and student life. At Penn, enrollment swelled to over 10,000 for the first time. In 1922, alumni of the university pushed for the establishment of a graduate committee: the Musical Club of the University of Pennsylvania. This group followed the example set at Harvard University and oversaw all musical activities at the university, including the band. While the band previously had numerous student and professional directors, it was not until the group was under the baton of Dr. Adolph Vogel, formerly a cellist with the Philadelphia Orchestra, and the Combined Music Clubs first graduate manager Dr. George E. Nitzsche, that the Penn Band began to flourish.

1897 UNIVERSITY OF PENNSYLVANIA BAND. This picture shows the original 27 members of the group sitting on the steps of the Furness Building (now called the Fischer Fine Arts Library) on the Penn campus. From left to right in the first row are unidentified, ? Davis, ? Gregg, John Ammon, ? Seely, ? Seely, and unidentified. The remaining members include ? Holmes, ? Rice, ? Heyke, ? Milliken, ? Casalduc; A. Felix DuPont, ? Riddle, Sams Ogelsby, ? Smith, D. R. Dudley, and Horace Beck. Ben is standing in the back holding the flag. (Collections of the University of Pennsylvania Archives.)

THE DENTAL HALL, 1901. The Dental Hall was designed by architect Edgar M. Seeler and built in 1896. John E. Heyke, a dental student, was the first director of the band. Thanks to the permission of a dental professor named Dr. Essig, the group's first rehearsals were held in the Dental Hall basement. The Dental Hall was also conveniently situated adjacently to the newly built Franklin Field. Today the building is known as Hayden Hall. (Collections of the University of Pennsylvania Archives.)

JUNIOR BALCONY AT THE QUADRANGLE, 1901. Built in 1895, the Quadrangle was the first dormitory at the university's new location in West Philadelphia. A. Felix Dupont first played his cornet at this location in 1897, marking the beginning of the organization's history. Seen here is Junior Balcony, which overlooks the eastern portion of the dormitory. This location is named after the tradition of juniors watching events such as the Push Ball and pants fights. (*University of Pennsylvania Illustrated.*)

HOUSTON HALL, 1901. Houston Hall, built in 1896, was the nation's first student union. Before its construction, students had no common areas to assemble for social activities. In its first year of existence, the band performed at the site. Later in its history, the group would reside in the building, and until 1970, it would serve as home for the organization. (*University of Pennsylvania Illustrated.*)

Two

The March Kings

Marching bands of the early 20th century were firmly rooted in military traditions. Among the first American marching bands on record was the United States Marine Band in 1798. Through the first 60 years of its existence, the University of Pennsylvania Band mirrored that prototype in appearance and practice. It showcased military-style uniforms, flamboyant drum majors, and fast-paced precision marching and maneuvering. At times, the groups blended with student military training activities, such as the Student Army Training Corp (SATC), during periods of war.

By 1930, a senior band of over 100 pieces was eventually established, as well as a junior band of 40 to 50 members, which served as a feeder for the other band. Dr. George E. Nitzsche fund-raised thousands of dollars for new uniforms, overcoats, and shakos (feather-plumed hats) modeled after the military uniforms worn by the West Point cadets. In addition to becoming a fixture at athletic and campus events, the band performed frequently on radio, including the radio station WIP and national broadcasts on CBS. Nitzsche secured professional engagements at the Earle, the Keith, and the Stanley, which were prominent movie theaters in Philadelphia at the time, and the band performed for cumulative audiences estimated in the tens of thousands. Many of these concerts were recorded by RCA Victor and distributed worldwide.

Most notably, the Penn Band of the early 20th century had the opportunity to perform with some of greatest bandsmen of the day. Roland F. Seitz, an accomplished composer and bandsman, not only composed the famous *The University of Pennsylvania Band March* for the young organization in 1901, but also rehearsed and performed with the organization. On three separate occasions, Nitzsche made it possible for the group to perform with the renowned John Philip Sousa, whose last visit occurred weeks before his death. Dr. Adolph Vogel's friend Edwin Franko Goldman, who was regarded only second to Sousa in the early 20th century, composed the *Franklin Field March* for the band. By the 1940s, the Penn Band was firmly established as one of the finest units in the country.

GEORGE E. NITZSCHE (1874–1961), LL.B., 1898. Dr. George E. Nitzsche is shown here on campus, standing in front of Ivy Day stones outside of modern-day College Hall. Nitzsche was an alumnus of the university and served as its first director of public relations and recorder. He served as the first graduate manager of the Combined Music Clubs, and with his assistance and fund-raising savvy, the Penn Band thrived. (Collections of the University of Pennsylvania Archives.)

THE UNIVERSITY OF PENNSYLVANIA BAND MARCH, 1901. In 1901, the renowned composer Roland F. Seitz (1867–1946) of Glen Rock wrote the famous *The University of Pennsylvania Band March*. Not only did he rehearse the group for this composition, but he also actually performed with the group as a "ringer," or professional substitute. The march is generally regarded as one of the finest compositions ever written for a student band, and ultimately was adapted by many other organizations throughout the country.

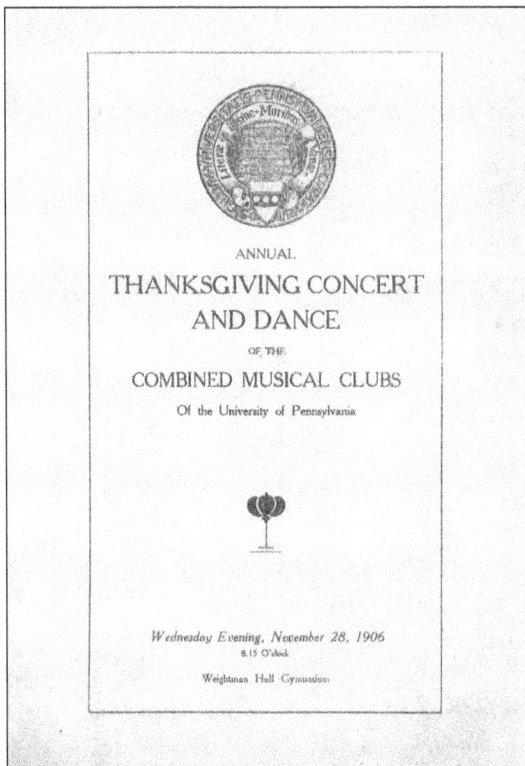

ANNUAL

THANKSGIVING CONCERT
AND DANCE

OF THE

COMBINED MUSICAL CLUBS

Of the University of Pennsylvania

Wednesday Evening, November 28, 1906
8.15 O'clock

Weightman Hall Gymnasium

COMBINED MUSIC CLUB PROGRAM, 1906. Pictured here is the cover of a program from a Thanksgiving event sponsored by the Combined Music Clubs. In the early 20th century, this organization included the Penn Glee Club, the Mandolin Club, and the Banjo Club. Eventually the Combined Music Club would disband in favor of a reorganized musical club in 1922.

THE BAND, 1919. Pictured here is the yearbook portrait of the 1919 band, posing on steps located in the Quadrangle. The uniforms were distinctly military in flavor. In jest, analogies were commonly drawn between the appearance of the band and the Salvation Army band. (*The Record*, 1919.)

THE PENN BAND OF THE EARLY 1930S. By the early 1930s, the size of the varsity band had swelled to nearly 100 members, as seen above. Shown below is the Penn Band in performance on Franklin Field, as the visiting band and cheerleaders watch. The identity of the other band is unknown.

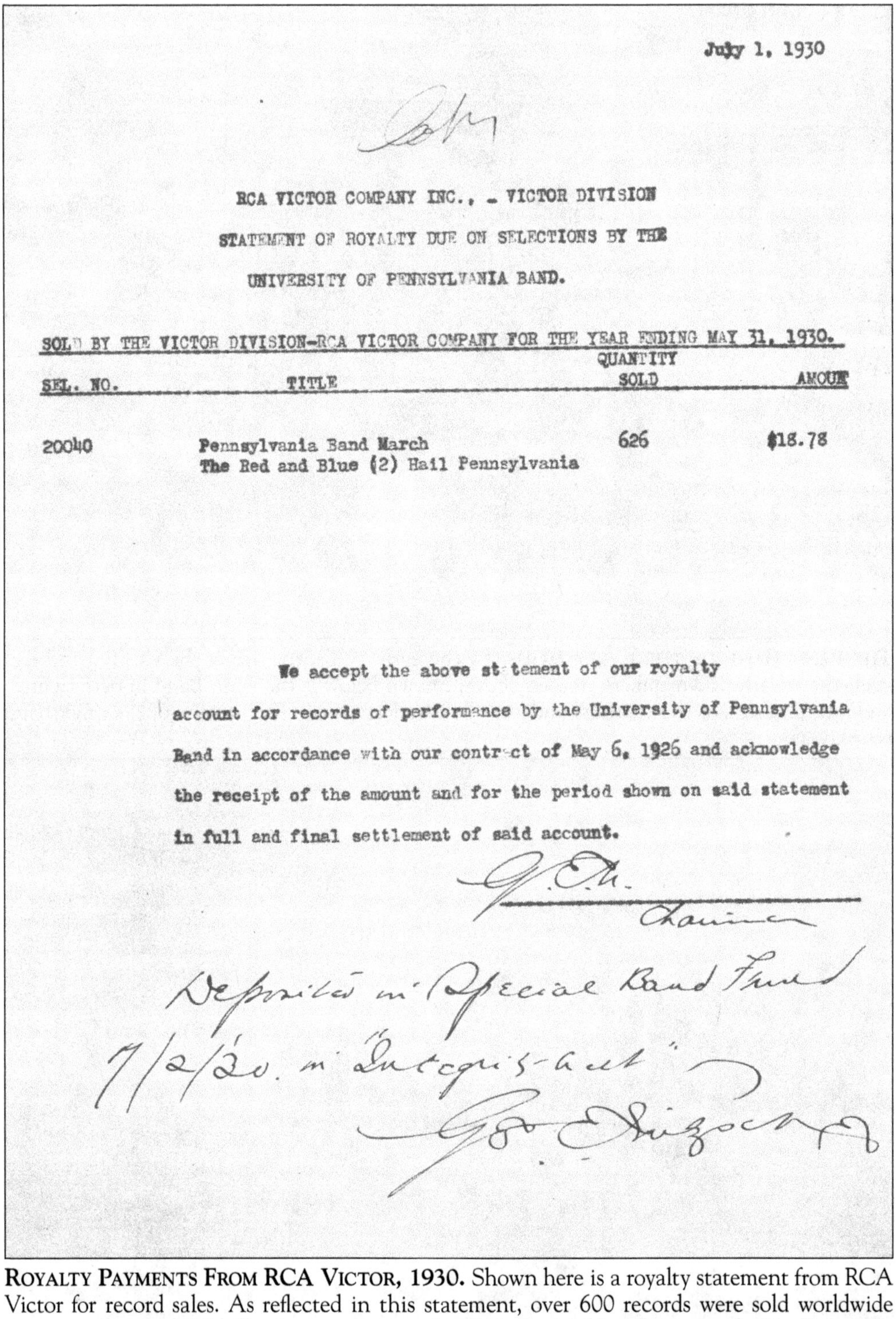

July 1, 1930

[signature]

RCA VICTOR COMPANY INC., _ VICTOR DIVISION

STATEMENT OF ROYALTY DUE ON SELECTIONS BY THE

UNIVERSITY OF PENNSYLVANIA BAND.

SOLD BY THE VICTOR DIVISION-RCA VICTOR COMPANY FOR THE YEAR ENDING MAY 31. 1930.

SEL. NO.	TITLE	QUANTITY SOLD	AMOUNT
20040	Pennsylvania Band March The Red and Blue (2) Hail Pennsylvania	626	$18.78

We accept the above statement of our royalty

account for records of performance by the University of Pennsylvania

Band in accordance with our contract of May 6, 1926 and acknowledge

the receipt of the amount and for the period shown on said statement

in full and final settlement of said account.

[signature] Chairman

[handwritten: Deposited in "Special Band Fund"]

[handwritten: 7/2/30. in "Incoquis-act"]

[signature]

ROYALTY PAYMENTS FROM RCA VICTOR, 1930. Shown here is a royalty statement from RCA Victor for record sales. As reflected in this statement, over 600 records were sold worldwide since its release in 1926. Funds earned were placed in a special band account by Dr. George E. Nitzsche and used to fund expenses such as uniforms and instruments. A large number of these records were sold in Japan. (Collections of the University of Pennsylvania Archives.)

DRUM MAJOR UNIFORM, 1920. The Penn Band drum major (unidentified) from 1920 is shown here in full uniform, including busby and mace. The busby added considerable height to the uniform. In 1923, the drum major known as "Shorty" Marsh stood as one of the tallest band drum majors known, at six feet seven inches tall. Wearing the uniform hat, he measured over eight feet in height. (Collections of the University of Pennsylvania Archives.)

THE PENN BAND AT LEHIGH UNIVERSITY, 1929. This picture depicts the Penn Band in performance at Lehigh University at a football game. In 1901, the Penn Band established the practice of not only performing at home contests, but also traveling to away games in support of its football team.

THE EARLE THEATRE, AROUND 1930. In addition to athletic contests, the Penn Band performed in prominent venues in Philadelphia. Nitzsche secured professional engagements at theaters such as the Earle, the Keith, and the Stanley. More than 70,000 people heard the Penn Band perform at the Stanley during the first week of December 1923. Seen here is one of the posters advertising the Penn Band's appearances at the Earle.

THE CROWD IN UNISON, 1933. The conductor leads the Penn Band in a rendition of the school song, *The Red and Blue*, in this picture. The crowd at Franklin Field and cheerleaders follow along. (*Fight on Pennsylvania: A Century of Red and Blue Football.*)

THE PENN BAND PERFORMS WITH JOHN PHILIP SOUSA. Above, on several occasions the famous John Philip Sousa conducted the Penn Band in performance. The last such occasion was on November 21, 1930, when he led the band in the concert in the Quadrangle. Below, Sousa received a gold medal from members of the group. From left to right are the following: Howard Berg, Lee Offut, Dary Dunham, and commander Sousa. Aside from his own marches, Sousa also had the opportunity to conduct *The University of Pennsylvania Band March*, after which he was quoted as saying, "That is one of the best band marches, aside from my own productions, I have ever conducted." At a luncheon in his honor afterwards, he suggested commemorating his next march to the group. Sousa passed away a few weeks later. (Collections of the University of Pennsylvania Archives.)

RELICS OF SOUSA'S LAST VISIT. Howard Berg (class of 1930, pictured on the previous page, standing to the left of commander Sousa) kindly donated the items pictured to the Penn Band in the mid-1980s, nearly 50 years after his time as an undergraduate. The hat (left), complete with feather plume, is the one Berg wore during his time with the Penn Band. The baton (below), all wood in construction, is the one Sousa used during his last performance with the group. Both relics currently reside in the office of the Penn Band. Hats stopped being a part of the band's appearance with the changes in uniform that came in the early 1960s.

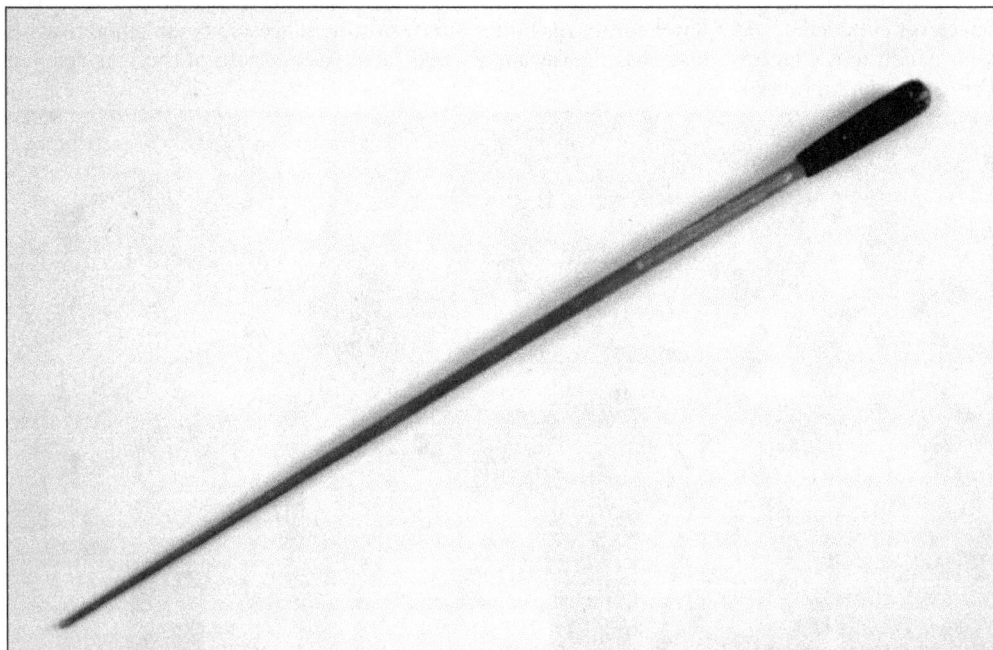

LUCIEN CAILLET (1891–1985). Lucien Caillet is pictured here performing with the Philadelphia Orchestra on his bass clarinet. During his time in Philadelphia, he created the Penn Band arrangements of *Fight On, Pennsylvania!*, *The Red and Blue*, and *Hang Jeff Davis* still used today. After his time in Philadelphia, he went on to have a successful career as a member of the faculty at the University of Southern California, as well as a career scoring films in Hollywood.

YEARBOOK PORTRAIT, 1939. Shown here is the band posing for a portrait on the steps of Houston Hall. In 1939, the Penn Band reorganized its leadership structure, doing away with the student manager position in favor of the elected positions of president, secretary, and treasurer. This governing body was named the Fanfare Honor Society. Today the body survives in the form of an honor society for band upperclassmen, a distinction awarded for service to the organization. (*The Record*, 1939.)

EDWIN FRANKO GOLDMAN (1878–1956). The famed bandsman is pictured here conducting the Penn Band in performance at Franklin Field. On November 5, 1932, Goldman's *Franklin Field March* was performed for the first time at the annual University of Pittsburgh–University of Pennsylvania football game. Goldman conducted the combined bands, numbering over 400 men and spreading over three-quarters of the field. (Collections of the University of Pennsylvania Archives.)

FRANKLIN FIELD, AROUND 1945. The historic stadium was built in 1895 for a cost of $100,000. The stadium was the site of the nation's first scoreboard (1895), the country's first two-tiered stadium (1922), the first football radio broadcast (WIP, 1922), and the first football telecast (PhilCo, 1939). (Collections of the University of Pennsylvania Archives.)

BACKWARD HATS, 1947. Pictured here is the band celebrating a football victory by parading around campus wearing their hats backwards. This was a tradition celebrated by Penn football enthusiasts during the height of Penn's football prominence. This photograph was taken shortly after the debut of new uniforms for the organization.

THE PENN BAND'S DRUMLINE ON FRANKLIN FIELD, 1947. In 1947, the band was outfitted with new uniforms that bore a strong military resemblance. At the time, the band was linked to Reserve Officer Training Corp (ROTC) training program, as World War II deeply affected enrollment and student activities at the university. Seen here are percussionists drumming the band off the field. (Photograph by George H. Roberts.)

SELLOUT CROWDS, 1947. Between the years 1938 and 1942, the football program led the country in home football attendance, averaging upwards of 80,000 attendees per game. Pictured in the upper image is a view, from the sidelines, of the band in a 1947 performance. Seen in the lower image is a view from Franklin Field's upper tier as the band performs for the audience in the north west corner of the stadium.

IN FORMATION, 1947. Pictured here is the Penn Band in different formations during halftime performances at Franklin Field, including a clock (above) and dollar sign (below). In the early 20th century, it became a common practice for marching bands to complement their music with relevant formations on the football field.

THE STUDENT LEADERSHIP, 1947. Above, the Penn Band is seen performing on Franklin Field, under the direction of drum major Samuel Lange. Below, a photograph shows the band performing in the stands. In the front left in uniform is student director William Holcome. Next to Holcome on the right is Samuel Lange. Lange was famous for tossing the baton over the goalpost and catching it before each game, as well as for twirling flaming batons.

A Tribute to Navy, 1947. The football series between the University of Pennsylvania and the Naval Academy began in 1888, and through the following 98 years was always a celebrated contest. Here the band is seen in formation, paying tribute to the visitors. Above, the band is in formation in the shape of an anchor. Below, the band is pictured in a more elaborate formation in the shape of a battleship. Seen in the stands behind the football field are entire sections of the stands at Franklin Field occupied by midshipmen.

CELEBRATING THE UNIVERSITY IN FORMATION, 1947. The Penn Band is show here in formation, spelling PENN (above) and U of P (below). Formations such as these are a trademark of the organization. It is not entirely clear which university marching band was the first to spell letters and words in formations on the football field. The Purdue University Band claims to have been the first band to form a letter on a field (a *P*), in 1907. The University of Illinois Band makes the claim to have been the first to spell words, in 1910.

DRILL SERGEANTS, AROUND 1945. Over the first half of the 20th century, several ROTC instructors conducted drills with the band. Sergeant Hammer (right) was one such instructor, who helped drill the Penn Band from 1942 to 1945 during World War II. In this picture, he is shown standing behind College Hall on campus. Below, the Penn Band is seen in parade block formation at the same location, with Sergeant Hammer standing to the right of the first rank. The building to the left is College Hall. The building to the right is Irvine Auditorium. (Right, photograph by George H. Roberts; below, collections of the University of Pennsylvania Archives.)

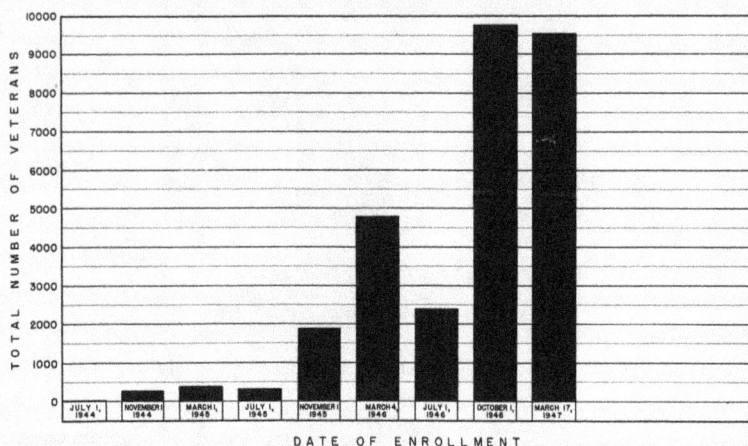

THE BOYS ARE BACK

University Postwar Enrollment. The end of World War II was not necessarily a boon for membership in the band, despite the increase in overall enrollment at the university. Many of the returning veterans who had been band members prior to their tour of duty did not continue as members of the band, as financial burdens and the need to complete coursework were higher priorities. Apparent in this illustration is the boom in university enrollment after the war. (Collections of the University of Pennsylvania Archives.)

The Tunnel, 1950s. The band forms a tunnel to greet the football team that is about to enter Franklin Field for competition. Also seen in this image are the drum major (unknown) and a cheerleader (unknown). (Collections of the University of Pennsylvania Archives.)

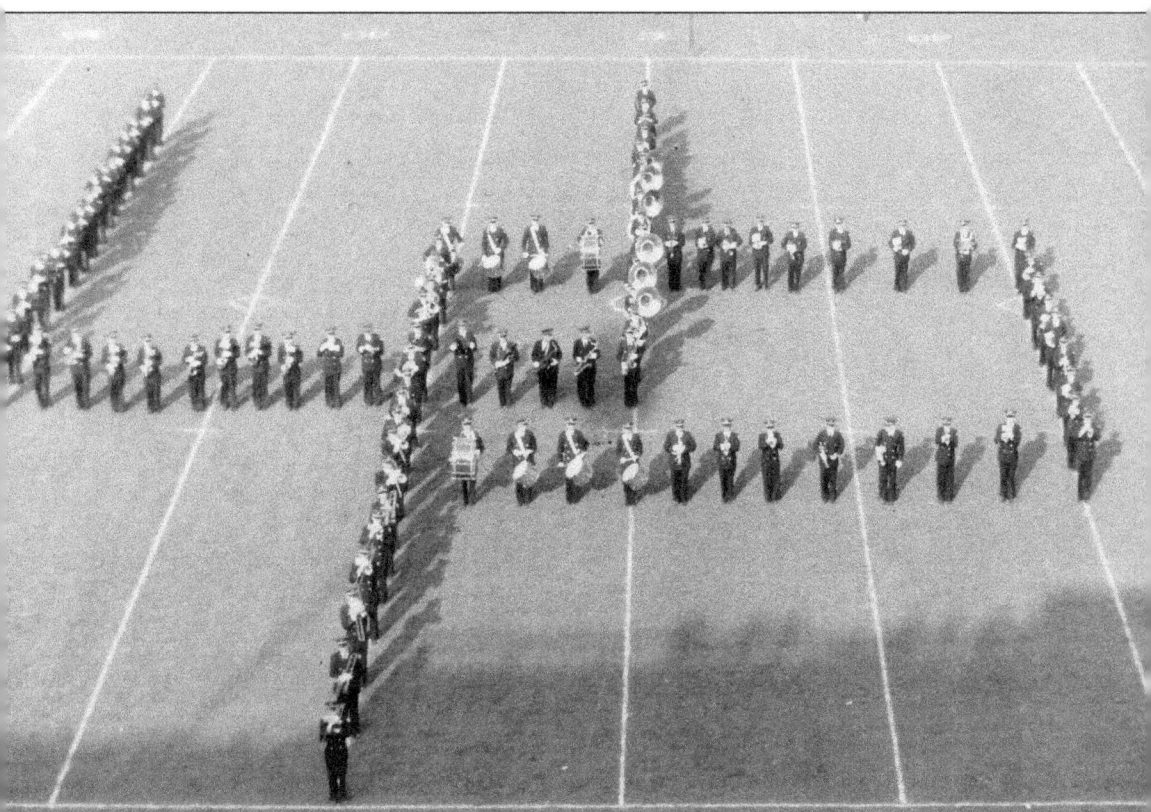

OVERLAPPING _U P_, AROUND 1947. The Penn Band forms a _U_ overlapping with a _P_ as it preforms _The Red and Blue._

UNDER STUDENT DIRECTION, 1947. Shown in this image is student director William Holcome leading the Penn Band on Franklin Field. Also seen is drum major Samuel Lange standing at attention.

THE CORNELL UNIVERSITY BAND, 1950S. For decades, the University of Pennsylvania–Cornell University football game (the final contest of the regular season) was played on Thanksgiving Day. In this photograph, the Cornell Band can be seen paying tribute to its hosts with the formation of a large P embedded in a football. (Collections of the University of Pennsylvania Archives.)

COVER OF PENN PICS, 1948. Shown here is the cover from a 1948 edition of *Penn Pics*, a student humor magazine. Appearing in the bottom right is the Penn Band in formation; above is an image of Warren Buffet, a university alumnus and prominent American businessman. The identity of the female to the right is unknown. (Collections of the University of Pennsylvania Archives.)

HALFTIME VERSUS ARMY, 1944. Seen here is the band finishing a halftime show with its rendition of *The Red and Blue*, as the football team waits to get back on the field. (*Fight on Pennsylvania: A Century of Red and Blue Football.*)

FROM HIGH ABOVE, 1950S. This is a panoramic view of Franklin Field, taken while the Penn Band performed at the pleasure of tens of thousands of fans. (Collections of the

University of Pennsylvania Archives.)

ONE MINUTE TOO EARLY, 1956. Euphoric fans celebrate the end of a 19-game Penn losing streak; the band can be seen to the left of the crowd. So overjoyed were the fans that they tore down the goalposts in celebration. Unfortunately, there was still one minute left on the game clock. (*Fight on Pennsylvania: A Century of Red and Blue Football.*)

WOODLAND WALK, 1958. On January 11, 1958, Woodland Avenue was officially closed between Thirty-fourth and Thirty-seventh Streets. University president Gaylord Harnwell is seen at the podium as the band (to the right) awaits its opportunity to perform. (Collections of the University of Pennsylvania Archives.)

Three

THE TRADITIONS OF
THE UNIVERSITY OF
PENNSYLVANIA

The new residential student community of the late 19th century in West Philadelphia created a diverse array of student activities. Including music and intercollegiate athletics, the activities became the centerpieces of the quintessential collegiate experience. Out of this community's annual cycle of athletic contests and class events, student traditions were established and perpetuated that live on today in the Penn community and are practiced and revered. The majority of unique traditions enjoyed by the University of Pennsylvania community today call upon student-written songs from the early part of the 20th century. This repertory is rich in colorful lyrics and melodies, and inextricably linked with many of the traditions of the student body.

Few musical outlets existed for students before the move to West Philadelphia; the only contemporary group in existence was the Penn Glee Club (established in 1862). After the move, the University Orchestra followed in 1878 and the Mask and Wig Club in 1889. Despite the scarcity of musical organizations, an active repertoire of class and event-specific songs did accumulate. However, it would not be until the establishment of the community in West Philadelphia, and the practices revolving around the emerging football phenomenon, that songs would persist and be forever etched into the school's canon. With the rise of intercollegiate football, Penn's popular fight songs were widely broadcasted, both at pep rallies and in the stands at contests. They were embraced by tens of thousands of spectators at Franklin Field and on campus. The advent of radio and commercialized television broadcasts of Penn football games further advanced the widespread familiarity of these fight songs. By 1909, in a revised version of the *Songs of Pennsylvania*, dozens of songs were presented. The vast majority of these songs bear little resemblance to the repertory of 1879 and more closely resemble the songs that are practiced today.

ALUMNI DAY. In 1887, alumni of the university established the practice of holding reunion events in conjunction with commencement exercises. Above, the band is seen at the 1912 event at Franklin Field. Below, the band is among several performing bands present at the 1919 event. (Collections of the University of Pennsylvania Archives.)

COLLABORATION WITH THE GLEE CLUB, 1954. Under the direction of Bruce C. Beach and Penn Glee Club director Robert Godsall, the band and glee club not only collaborated in concerts on campus, but also cooperated in the production of the record shown here, a compilation of the most popular Penn fight songs.

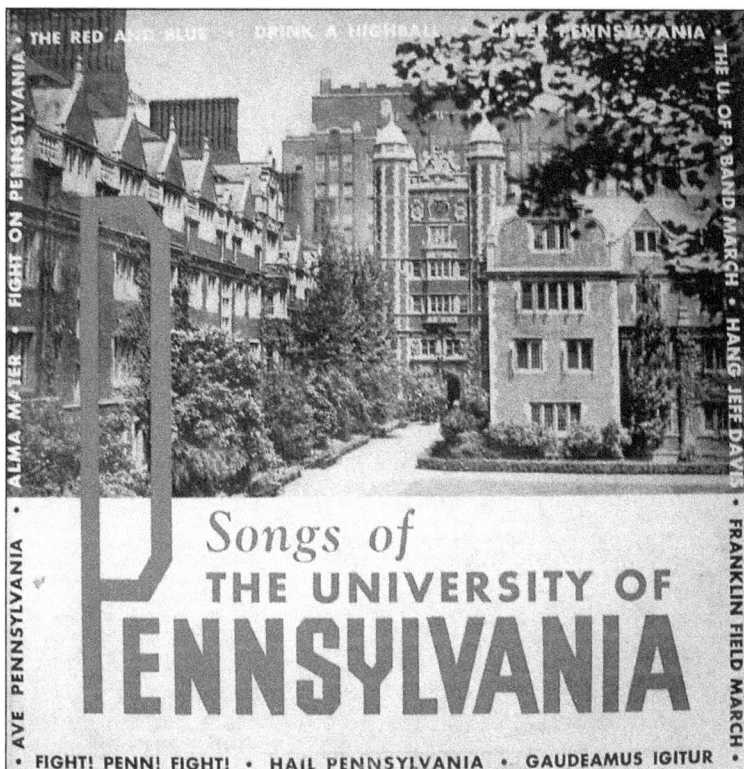

Songs of
THE UNIVERSITY OF
PENNSYLVANIA

• FIGHT! PENN! FIGHT! • HAIL PENNSYLVANIA • GAUDEAMUS IGITUR •

BICENTENNIAL
SONGS

1740   1940

University
of
Pennsylvania

THORNTON W. ALLEN
COMPANY
New York, N.Y.

THE UNIVERSITY OF PENNSYLVANIA BICENTENNIAL, MARCH 1940. To celebrate the bicentennial of the university, a competition was held for a song to celebrate the occasion. The winning submission was written by Edward Foley (class of 1935), with lyrics written by Robert A. Doane (class of 1942). Shown here is the cover art to a collection of songs released during the bicentennial celebration, which includes the winning submission: *The University of Pennsylvania Bicentennial March.*

43

ALMA MATER OF THE UNIVERSITY OF PENNSYLVANIA, 1985. *Hail Pennsylvania* is a tune by Edgar M. Dilley (class of 1897), based on the Russian national anthem. Seen here is the band at the homecoming football game in 1985, in a traditional "Big P" formation.

FIELD CRY OF PENNSYLVANIA (HANG JEFF DAVIS), 1947. This song has traditionally been sung after every touchdown at Penn football games. Pictured here is the Penn Band in a formation of a platform with a noose, while preforming the song. The *Field Cry of Pennsylvania* is sung to the Civil War–era tune *John Brown's Body*. It is unknown who adapted the lyrics to this contemporary version. Morrison C. Boyd (class of 1913) is credited with arranging this song for performance.

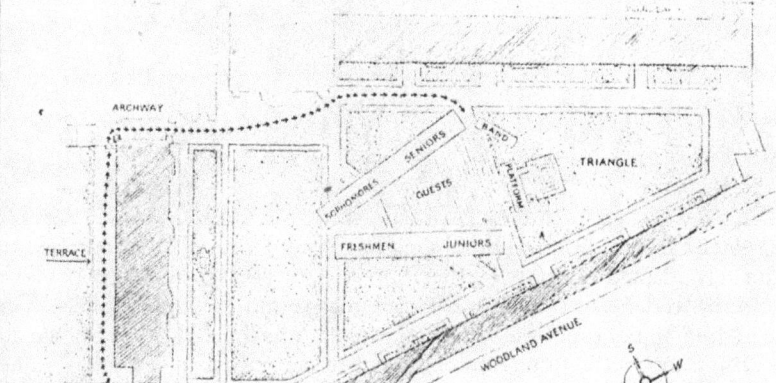

THE DAILY PENNSYLVANIAN

PHILADELPHIA, WEDNESDAY, MAY 12, 1937

PLAN OF HEY DAY EXERCISES

ARCHWAY

SENIORS

BAND

PLATFORM

TRIANGLE

SOPHOMORES

GUESTS

TERRACE

FRESHMEN

JUNIORS

WOODLAND AVENUE

HEY DAY. Hey Day is a tradition celebrated by undergraduate juniors. It began in 1916 and is modeled after a ritual established at Syracuse University. In 1937, a parade of Penn's junior class, led by the Penn Band, was introduced as part of the event. Shown above is a map of the parade route during its first year, as it appeared in the student newspaper. Seen below is a more contemporary image of the event as it was in 1990, with the Penn Band leading the parade. The Penn Band remains involved in the parade to this day. (Above, collections of the University of Pennsylvania Archives; below, courtesy of Brian Greenberg, class of 1990.)

DRINK A HIGHBALL. This traditional school song was derived from a British barracks tune. This song was ultimately adapted not only by the Penn student body in the early part of the 20th century, but also by students at the University of Chicago and Wesleyan College. The student band performed this popular tune at football games as early as the mid-1920s. Shown above is an image of the Penn Band in the formation of a highball beverage from a football game in 1947. Below, a variation of the same formation is shown from a 1976 football game at Franklin Field.

HIGHBALL GLASSES. Ironically, true highball glasses are long cylinders, not shaped like a wine or martini glass as in the 1964 formations pictured above. Another feature characteristic of the highball formation over the years is the "draining of the glass" as the song proceeds, by the forward advancement of the rank of band members "in" the glass during the course of the song. The picture at right is from 1985.

RED AND BLUE: SCOTTISCHE ELEGANTE, 1905. Before the rise of the student band, glee club, records, and the radio, the most common medium for music was in the form of piano sheet music. After the composition of the school song *The Red and Blue* by William Goeckel (class of 1895) and Dr. Harry E. Westervelt (class of 1898), another composition by John C. Simpson carried a similar title, as shown at left.

AT VAN PELT LIBRARY, LATE 1960s. Several years after the composition of *The Red and Blue*, standing and waving hats in time with the chorus of the tune became popular. Shown here is the Penn Band and cheerleaders practicing this tradition in the late 1960s on the steps of Van Pelt Library. This practice still survives today and stands as one of the campus's most revered traditions. (Photograph by John Keplinger.)

48

THE RED AND BLUE AT FRANKLIN FIELD, 1947. Pictured here is the band performing *The Red and Blue* at Franklin Field. In this formation, the members standing in the shield in the upper photograph drop their hats and move back into the *P* formation, leaving the outline of hats seen in the lower image.

THE RED AND BLUE IN A BLOCK FORMATION, 1947. In this image, the Penn Band performs the chorus to *The Red and Blue* at Franklin Field. The drum major and cheerleaders can be seen waving their arms to the chorus of the tune.

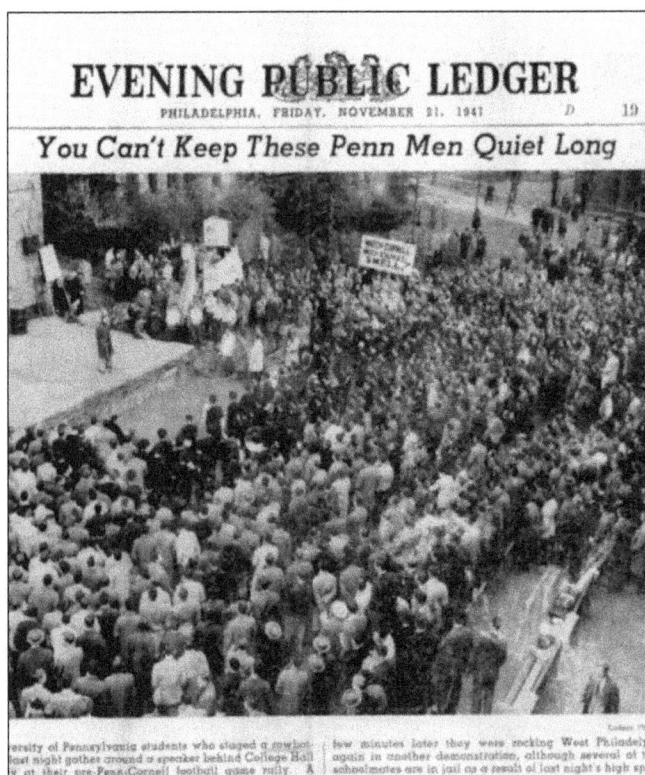

EVENING PUBLIC LEDGER

PHILADELPHIA, FRIDAY, NOVEMBER 21, 1941   D   19

You Can't Keep These Penn Men Quiet Long

ROWBOTTOM, 1941. The "Rowbottom" was an unusual tradition of mass student disturbances and riots that has long since past from regular practice. In this ritual, one would yell, "Hey Rowbottom!" to summon the spirit of 1913 graduate Jonathan Tintsman Rowbottom, initiating the mayhem. The image shown here from *The Evening Public Ledger* shows the band at the center of a pep rally that took place behind College Hall before the annual University of Pennsylvania–Cornell University football game in 1941. The rally ended in a Rowbottom. It is unknown how the band fared during the riot. (Collections of the University of Pennsylvania Archives.)

50

SCRIPT PENN, 1986. Beginning in the 1970s, the band started a football homecoming tradition of spelling PENN in cursive script before its rendition of *The Red and Blue*. Seen here is that formation presented by the 1986 band at Franklin Field.

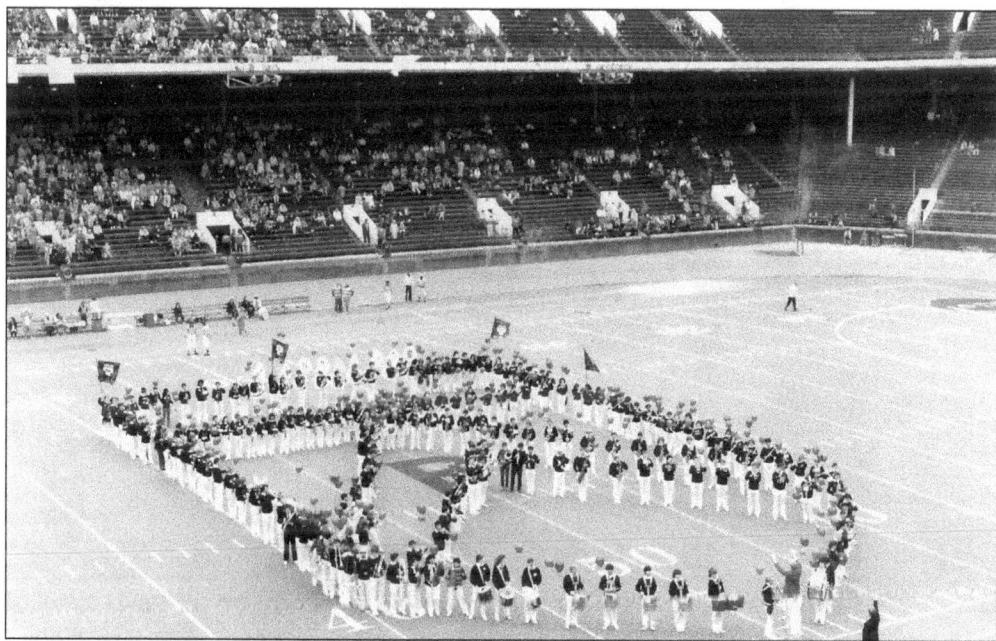

THE SHIELD, 1986. This formation made its premiere at a football game in 1985, in lieu of the P formation, for the performance of *Hail Pennsylvania*. This shield has been a traditional part of the university's identity for many decades.

***FIGHT ON, PENNSYLVANIA!*, 1969.** At the age of 17, David Zoob (class of 1923) wrote the school fight song *Fight On, Pennsylvania!*; Ben McGiveran (class of 1923) added the lyrics. This creation would become the centerpiece of the canon of Penn songs and arguably one of the greatest college fight songs ever written. In November 1969, Zoob was honored by university president Gaylord Harnwell at halftime with the presentation of a watch. Zoob then conducted the Penn Band in a rendition of the song to mark its 50th anniversary. (Collections of the University of Pennsylvania Archives.)

DIXIE GROUP AT SKIMMER, 1955. The Skimmer student tradition began in 1949 and continued until 1973, ultimately replaced by Spring Fling. The celebration was marked by social, musical, and athletic events along the Schuylkill River and on campus. Seen here is an ensemble of instrumentalists performing for the students at Skimmer in 1955. (Collections of the University of Pennsylvania Archives.)

Four

THE UNIVERSITY OF PENNSYLVANIA BANDS

In 1954, the presidents of the Ivy-League schools revised the agreement previously established in 1945, establishing the Ivy League. This formally extended academic, financial, and athletic standards to all intercollegiate athletics within the conference. The loss of academic scholarships and limits on athletics spending had a profound effect on the football program at the university.

In addition to these fundamental changes, there were changing attitudes towards the military tradition. With the end of World War II and the "return to normalcy, " the focus of military training on campus and its influence on the marching band were diminished. The number of women and African Americans enrolled at the university increased, further altering the social dynamic of the student body.

In turn, the organization's essence changed, and these alterations began on the football field. Abandoned were the military-style uniforms that were characteristic of its first 50 years of existence. Also the Penn Band had a change of style, which was marked by the adoption of red blazers, white shirts, and black ties. Gradually the group introduced more satire and wit into its halftime shows, beginning its transformation into a scramble band. Instead of serving primarily as a football marching band, the group developed a broader scope of performance. The musical tradition, not the military tradition, became the focus. Born out of the organization were a symphonic band, a jazz band, a pep band, a brass ensemble, and a Dixie band. The group had transformed and diversified into the University of Pennsylvania Bands, an umbrella organization for student instrumental performance.

During the 1960s, the organization thrived under the baton of directors such as Joseph A. Colontanio and E. Dennis Rittenhouse. In concert, the organization performed at a professional level and collaborated with artists such as Carl Hilding "Doc" Severinson, Vaclav Nelhybel, and others.

GROUP PORTRAIT OF THE PENN BAND, EARLY 1960s. This is the last known portrait of the band in military-style uniform. (Collections of the University of Pennsylvania Archives.)

THE PENN BAND ON JUNIOR BALCONY, 1960s. Here the band is seen leaving Junior Balcony in the Quadrangle after a performance. This football-day tradition continues today.

PERFORMING AT NIGHT. Seen in these images is the band performing at night on campus in the 1960s. Seen most clearly in the lower image is the uniform that distinguished the band of the 1960s from previous decades: a red logo blazer, black pants, and a white shirt with a tie. (Photographs by John Keplinger.)

THE PALESTRA, 1927. The Palestra was built in 1927 and stands as one of college basketball's most historic gymnasia. It was not long after its construction that the band began performing regularly at athletic events in the venue. (Collections of the University of Pennsylvania Archives.)

THE PEP BAND, 1960s. One of the many extensions of the University of Pennsylvania Bands was a pep band that performed at the men's basketball games. Shown in this image is the band finding its seats at a crowded basketball game at the Palestra.

56

RECRUITING A PEP BAND, 1960s. This advertisement appeared in the student paper in the early 1960s, with the objective of recruiting students for the basketball pep band.

THE UNIVERSITY OF PENNSYLVANIA BANDS

ANNOUNCE

THE FORMATION OF A PEP BAND
OF 20 TO 30 WINDS AND PERCUSSION
TO PERFORM AT ALL HOME AND SELECTED
AWAY GAMES
OF THE VARSITY BASKETBALL TEAM

*OPEN TO ALL FACULTY, GRADUATE AND
UNDERGRADUATE STUDENTS*

*FREE ADMISSION FOR YOU AND YOUR DATE
TO ALL GAMES*

CONTACT
THE BAND OFFICE BEFORE
NOVEMBER 26
SECOND FLOOR EAST,
HOUSTON HALL,
EXTENSION 8719

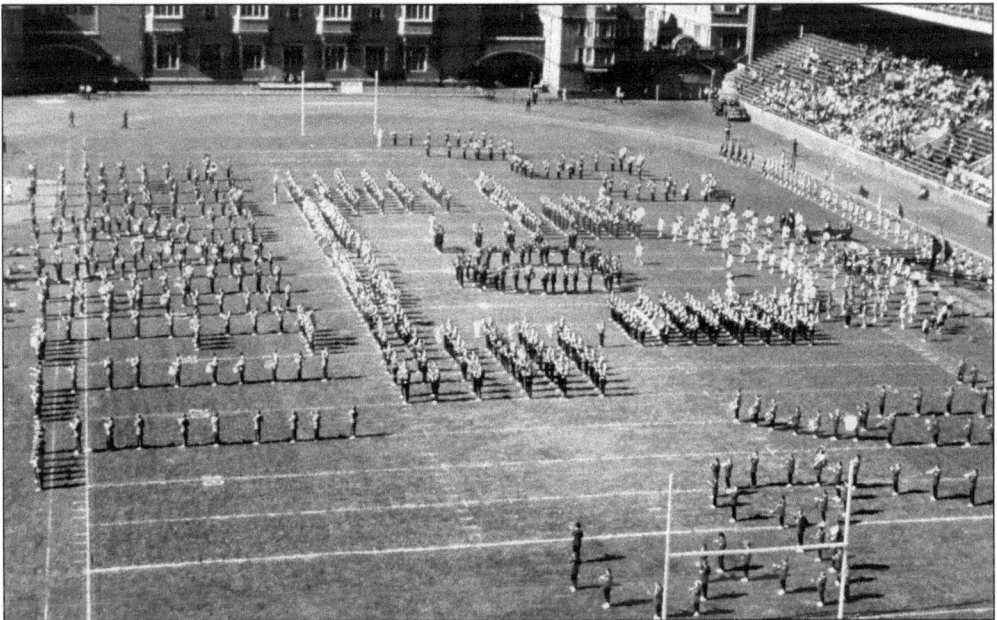

BAND DAY, 1965. In 1936, Penn's School of Education started the Cultural Olympics, an event designed to promote arts in local schools; the Penn Band participated in the organization of Band Day. This event would often draw several hundred participating students. At one such Band Day in the 1930s, an astonishing 3,600 students were assembled on Franklin Field. Shown in this image is the Penn Band Day held in 1965, where over 600 students were assembled.

CONCERT ON THE GREEN. The band can be seen in these images from the 1960s performing at concerts in what is now known as Blanche P. Levy Park, then known as the Green, which is the park that lies at the center of campus between College Hall and Van Pelt Library. This tradition continues to today. In the lower image, the Penn Band can be seen under the baton of E. Dennis Rittenhouse.

THE SYMPHONIC BAND. After the completion of football season, the focus of the Penn Band's schedule would shift to the symphonic band and indoor performance. The Penn Band had reciprocal concert agreements with other universities, in addition to performing with frequency on the Penn campus. The concert poster shown here advertises one such concert in 1963, where the group performed with Bram Smith, a cornetist formerly of the United States Marine Band.

SHOWTIME '63

FEATURING

The

UNIVERSITY of PENNSYLVANIA
B A N D S

JOSEPH A. COLANTONIO, DIRECTOR

WITH

BRAM SMITH

Former Cornet Soloist with U.S. Marine Band

TOWN HALL
BROAD & RACE STREETS
PHILADELPHIA

SATURDAY, JANUARY 26th, 1963

8:30 p. m.

presenting...

THE
UNIVERSITY
OF
PENNSYLVANIA
BAND

ALLEN P. BUDER
BENEFIT CONCERT
SUNDAY AFTERNOON
FEBRUARY 7th - 2:00 P.M.
IRVINE AUDITORIUM

TICKETS AVAILABLE AT
HOUSTON HALL DESK
PI LAMBDA PHI – BA 2-9373
BAND OFFICE –H. H. 594-8719

donation
$1.50

ALLEN P. BUDER BENEFIT CONCERT, 1965. In 1965, Penn student Allen P. Buder died from injuries sustained at the University of Pennsylvania–Harvard University junior-varsity football game. Together with Pi Lambda Phi, the Penn Band sponsored a concert in his memory. The proceeds benefited a special financial aid fund at the University of Pennsylvania.

59

Spring Festival '64

FEATURING

THE

Symphonic Band

OF THE

UNIVERSITY of PENNSYLVANIA

JOSEPH A. COLANTONIO, DIRECTOR

WITH

VACLAV NELHYBEL, GUEST CONDUCTOR

IRVINE AUDITORIUM
34th & SPRUCE STREETS
PHILADELPHIA

SATURDAY, MARCH 21st, 1964

8:30 p. m.

VACLAV NELHYBEL, 1964. In 1964, the Penn Band performed with the internationally renowned eastern European composer Vaclav Nelhybel. The famed musician's visit coincided with a political symposium on campus that focused on eastern European politics. (Collections of the University of Pennsylvania Archives.)

UNDER THE BATON OF JOSEPH A. COLONTANIO, 1963. Pictured here is director Joseph A. Colontanio conducting the Penn Band at Franklin Field. Noteworthy is the drop in attendance in the background, in contrast with the sellout crowds observed in previous decades.

60

DIXIELAND BAND, 1968. One of many ensembles born out of the group was a Dixie-style ensemble. Seen here is that ensemble performing at a concert on Parris Island, South Carolina. This concert was part of a tour through the southern United States.

IN CONCERT, 1968. Seen in this image is the symphonic band in concert.

DREARY WEATHER. One of the several ensembles formed with the advent of the Combined Music Clubs of 1922 was a jazz orchestra. Surprisingly that ensemble was short-lived, as many of the most serious jazz musicians were occupied with paid engagements with dance bands on their weekends. Shown here is the cover art to a composition from one such dance band comprised of Penn students.

THE JAZZ BAND, 1964. In 1964, under the direction of Joseph A. Colontanio (seen to the left, directing the ensemble), the Penn Band premiered a jazz band at Houston Hall.

JAZZ BAND. The jazz band ensemble, which began in 1964, remained a part of the University of Pennsylvania Bands until 1974, when it became an autonomous student group. One of the highlights for the organization (along with the symphonic band) was a clinic and concert with Carl Hilding "Doc" Severinson of the *Tonight Show* band in 1967. It is interesting to note that despite a different context of performance, the group commonly used the same uniform used by the marching band, as seen in the lower image.

TWO CLARINETISTS. Pictured here are Kenneth Guttenplan (left) and an unidentified band member playing their clarinets in the late 1960s.

MILITARY TRIBUTE. Seen here is the Penn Band paying tribute to the armed forces in the 1960s, with many branches of the military participating in the formation on Franklin Field.

ON THE FIELD, 1960S. Above, the Penn Band enters the field, in a parade block, for performance. Below, the cymbalists are seen showcasing their instruments while the drum major stands at attention.

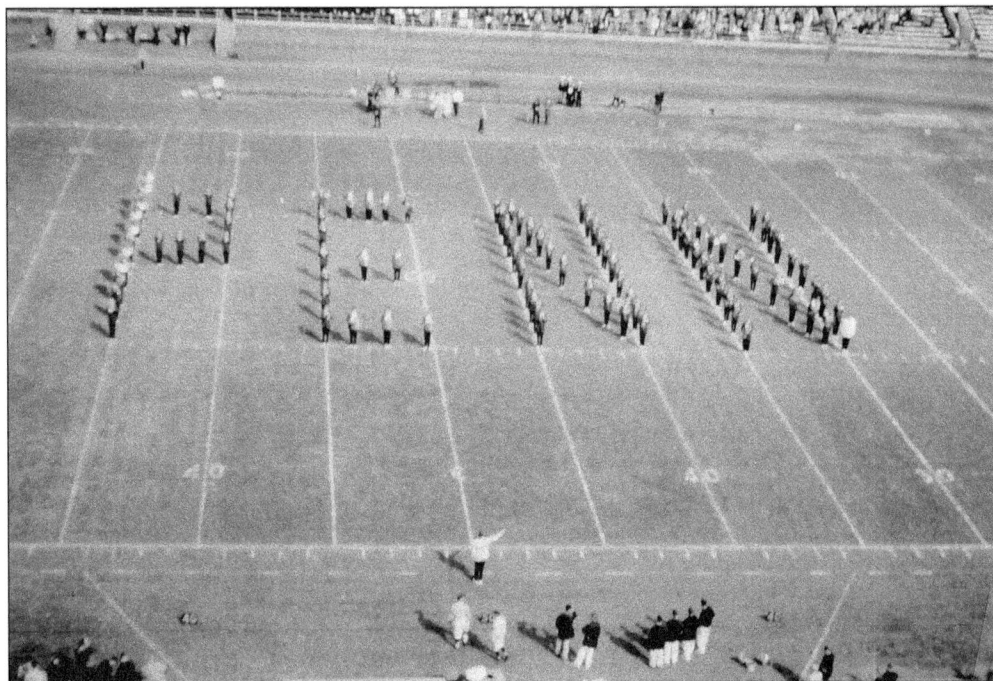

THE BAND, 1964. The 1964 band is shown above in a traditional PENN formation on Franklin Field. Below, the Penn Band makes a rare error, accidentally misplacing the letter *P* in PENN by five yards.

IN REHEARSAL, 1960S. The Penn Band is seen here in rehearsal at Hutchinson Gymnasium in the athletics complex.

these presentations ranges from the classics and contemporary band works to the scores from hit shows and movies. The concert season culminates with Musical Activities Night which showcases all of the musical groups on campus.

There are many smaller groups which have grown from the marching and concert ensembles. The first is the Quaker Stage Band. With a wide-range jazz repertoire, the stage band presents a campus concert each year in addition to performing at dances and activities in the Philadelphia area. The second group is the Penn Pep Band, alias, the Marajuana Brass. They add musical excitement and school spirit to the basketball madness that is Penn's Palestra.

So, look at the pictures, read the fine print, and decide. We're sure that you will want to partake of the friendly spirit and wholesome endeavor that have made the Penn Bands the snappiest activity on campus!

For further information, write:

Director
University of Pennsylvania Bands
Houston Hall
3417 Spruce Street
Philadelphia, Pennsylvania 19104

THE UNIVERSITY OF PENNSYLVANIA BANDS

PENN'S MOST PROGRESSIVE TRADITION

The University of Pennsylvania Bands offer musically inclined students a host of varied experiences.

Come September, the all-male Quaker Marching Band packs off for band camp in the Pocono Mountains to prepare precision drill routines for the approaching football season. Only a few

RECRUITING BROCHURE, AROUND 1965. This recruiting brochure from around 1965 described the Penn Band as one of Penn's "most progressive traditions." Also described is a brass ensemble playfully named "Marijuana Brass." This brass ensemble would later be called Top Brass.

...ays into the school year finds the band performing prior to the nationally televised United Nations Handicap at the Atlantic City Race Track.

Soon football season is here and the band drums up school spirit by leading a parade around campus climaxed by the annual pre-season pep rally. The pigskin campaign finds the band present at all home and most away games, leading the Penn cheering section and providing colorful and exciting pre-game and half-time shows. Every Quaker score results in a chorus of "Hang Jeff Davis" and each win is celebrated with a victory parade around campus, ending with a rally outside Houston Hall, the student union. The highlight of the football season is the annual Franklin Field Pageant of Bands, when the best high school bands in the Delaware Valley compete for highest awards in musical performance and marching.

The close of football season does not end the

marching band activities for the year. Recent years have found the band appearing in several holiday parades in the East. In fact, the Quaker Marching Band was the first college band to appear in the famous Macy's Thanksgiving Day Parade.

As the marching season ends, the addition of female musicians and a change in instrumentation transforms the marching band into the Symphonic Winds. During the past few years this group has travelled along the entire East coast from Maine to Florida. A recent tour of eight southern states was received by enthusiastic and appreciative audiences everywhere. In 1964, this group helped open the New York World's Fair and later returned to present concerts at the General Motors and General Cigar pavilions.

The Symphonic Winds also presents two concerts on campus each year. The bill of fare for

THE LINE, 1960s. The Penn Band prepares to enter Franklin Field for performance, forming a contiguous line along the end zone.

THE ANNENBERG CENTER FOR THE PERFORMING ARTS, 1970. Prior to the completion of the Annenberg Center for the Performing Arts, the Penn Band resided in Houston Hall. In 1970, the $4.2 million Annenberg Center became its new home, as Annenberg was designed to serve all performing arts on campus. This building provided a home for the program until the fall of 2006, when the Platt Student Performing Arts Center opened on campus. (Collections of the University of Pennsylvania Archives.)

Five

THE TRAVELING BAND

The loyalty of the Penn Band to its alma mater is matched by its love for travel. In 1901, the band traveled to its first away football game at Harvard University, establishing a precedent followed to this day. In this regard, the organization was a leader, as rarely did marching bands follow their respective football teams to away games at this time.

Travel was not always a convenient proposition for the group in its earliest years. Despite daunting distances with limited conveniences, the organization made trips to destinations such as the University of California in 1925 and the University of Michigan in 1940. It is said that while traveling to a football game on one occasion, some members had to sell their instruments in order for the group to afford the trip back to Philadelphia. On another occasion during the early 1970s, members disembarking from their buses upon arrival at Harvard Yard were met by the Cambridge police in full riot gear: the Penn Band was, in fact, mistaken for a group of protesters.

The group's travel has not been limited to sporting events over its history. By the 1950s, it became common practice for the organization to retreat to the Poconos in the late summer to learn halftime drills for the coming season. On the national stage, the organization toured the eastern seaboard with regularity, performing at events such as the 1964 New York World's Fair, the Miss America Pageant parade, and the Macy's Thanksgiving Day Parade on three separate occasions.

By the early 1980s, travel to football and men's basketball games was an established practice. On some occasions during this decade, the organization would take as many as four charter buses of members to an away football game. The band stands as one of the few, if not the only, college bands nationwide to travel to all home and away conference men's basketball games.

THE PENN BAND IN CALIFORNIA, 1925. The football team played the University of California three times during the 1920s, twice in the state of California. Pictured here is the Penn Band performing in front of thousands of fans at the University of California. (Collections of the University of Pennsylvania Archives.)

TRIP TO THE UNIVERSITY OF MICHIGAN, 1940. Pictured here are members of the Penn Band traveling to Ann Arbor, Michigan, for a football game between the University of Pennsylvania and the University of Michigan. In 1953, the members of the Penn Band voted to strike before relenting when a similar trip to Ann Arbor was not funded by the administration.

ON THE WAY TO THE POCONOS, LATE 1960S. Between the 1950s and 1960s, the Penn Band made the habit of retreating to the Poconos before the start of each football season to learn halftime drills, rehearse, and for recreation. Seen here are three members en route to the Poconos, bass drum in tow.

THE UNIVERSITY OF PENNSYLVANIA BAND AT THE 1964 WORLD'S FAIR IN NEW YORK. On April 22, 1964, the University of Pennsylvania Band appeared on national television in the parade that opened the festivities for the world's fair in Flushing Meadows, New York. The organization performed for Pres. Lyndon B. Johnson, both during the parade and in concert afterwards.

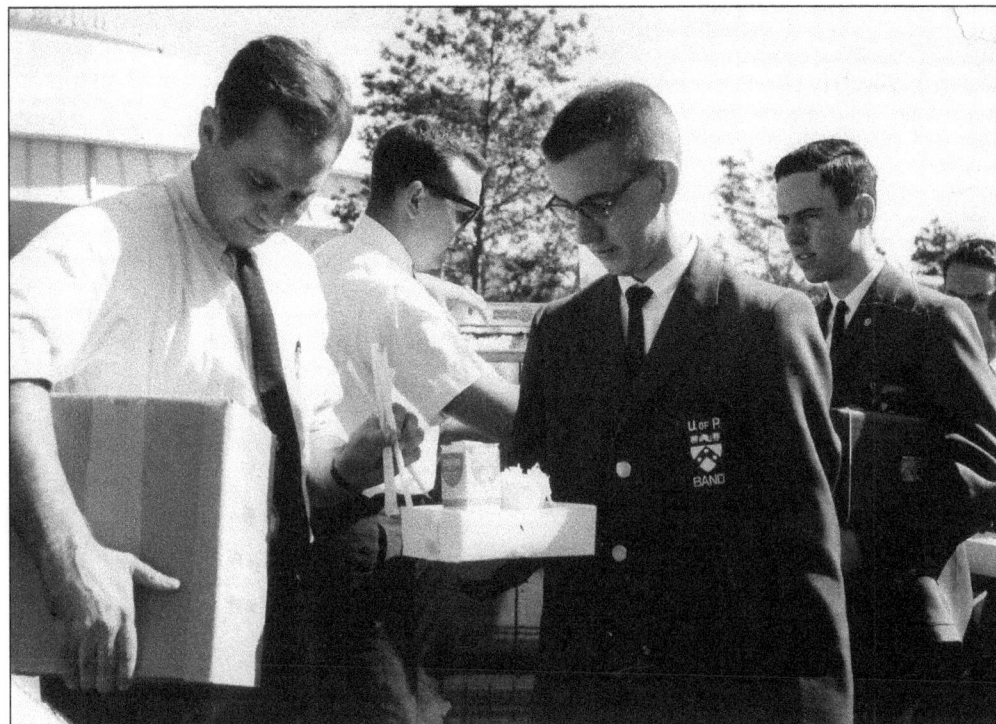

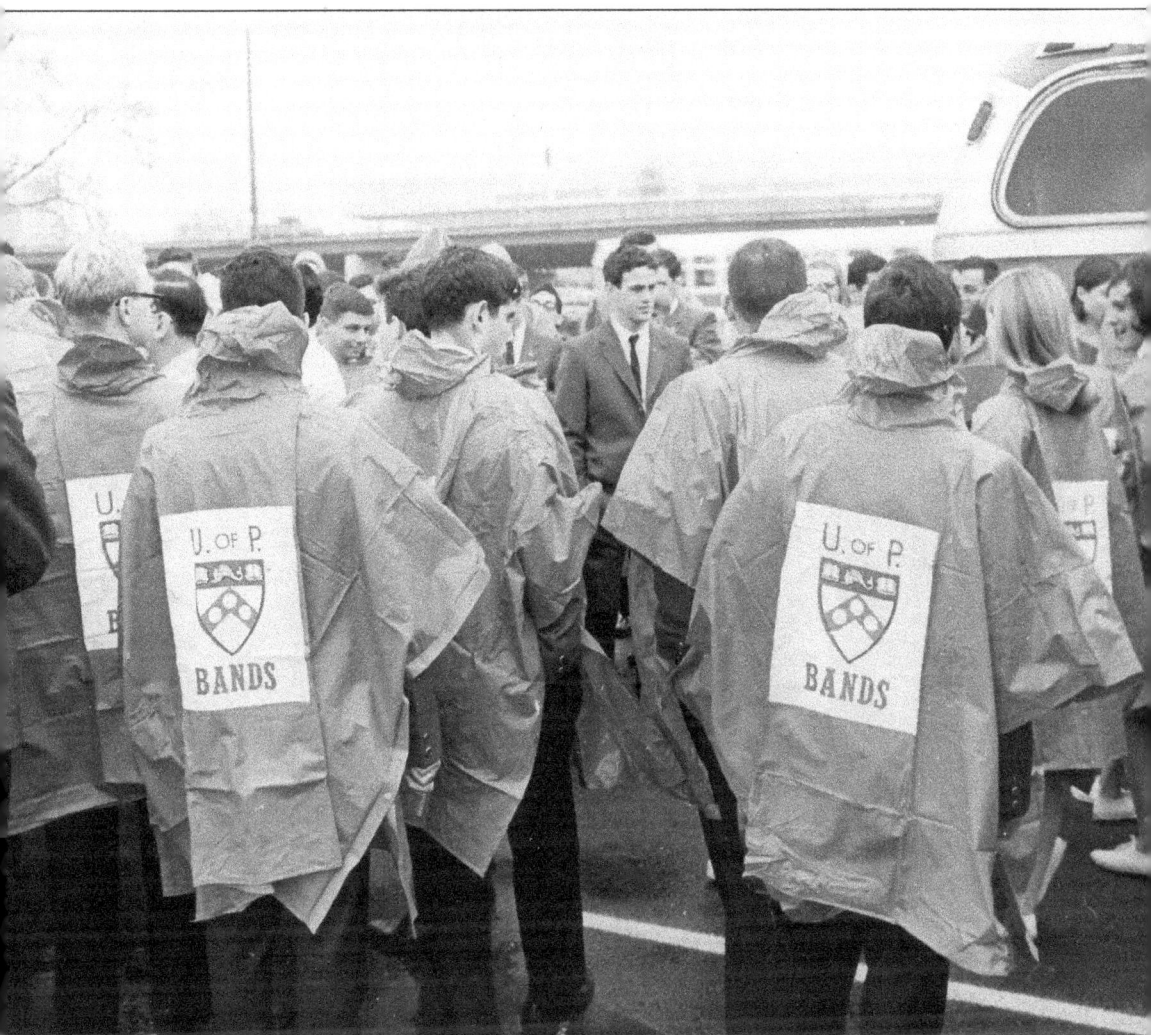

PLAYING IN THE RAIN, 1964. Members of the Penn Band don rain parkas in prelude to the New York World's Fair parade.

THE MACY'S THANKSGIVING DAY PARADE. The Penn Band was the first collegiate marching band ever to march in the prestigious Macy's parade in New York City. The group participated in the parade in 1962, 1963, and 1967. In 1967, the parade was nationally televised by NBC.

1967 MACY'S PARADE TROPHY. Shown here is the trophy received by the group after its performance in the 1967 Macy's Thanksgiving Day Parade. After the parade in 1967, the Penn Band boarded a bus and made it back to Philadelphia in time for the University of Pennsylvania–Cornell University football game. What makes this effort more remarkable is the fact that only about half of the 87 or so bandsmen marched in the parade, as the other half were in the hotel recovering from the flu.

LIBERTY BELL PARK, 1967. Above, the Penn Band performs at the Liberty Bell Park in Philadelphia, actually parading around the track. Below, the Penn Band performs on the track as another marching unit passes. (Photographs by John Keplinger.)

PARRIS ISLAND, 1968. The symphonic band is shown above in concert at Parris Island. At left, a bass drummer tends to his part. This performance was part of a larger winter trip that took the band through the states of Virginia, North Carolina, Georgia, and Florida. The band performed not only at the Marine Recruit Base at Parris Island, but also at the Fort Stewart United States Army base in Georgia and at several high schools. (Photographs by John Keplinger.)

BUS ARRIVAL, LATE 1960S. Members disembark from their buses after arriving at their destination (unknown). (Photograph by John Keplinger.)

THE 1974 GAS CRISIS. As a result of soaring fuel prices, the Penn Band's annual tour across the state of Pennsylvania, including visits to cities, schools, nursing homes, and veteran's hospitals, was cancelled.

THE NCAA MEN'S BASKETBALL FINAL FOUR, 1979. In the spring of 1979, the Pennsylvania Quakers upset two higher-seeded teams in Greensboro, North Carolina, en route to the Final Four in Utah, where the team ultimately fell to Michigan State University. During this improbable run, the Penn Band followed the team from game to game. (Courtesy of Vincent Palusci, class of 1980.)

TOO MANY BAND MEMBERS, 1987. In 1987, the Yale University Athletic Department imposed a restriction on the number of visiting Penn Band members who could perform at a men's basketball game. In adherence to these rules, the first 20 instrumentalists wore identification tags; the remaining 26 members on the trip had to buy tickets and were not permitted to play their instruments. In protest, these 26 other members of the Penn Band "played" cardboard mock instruments.

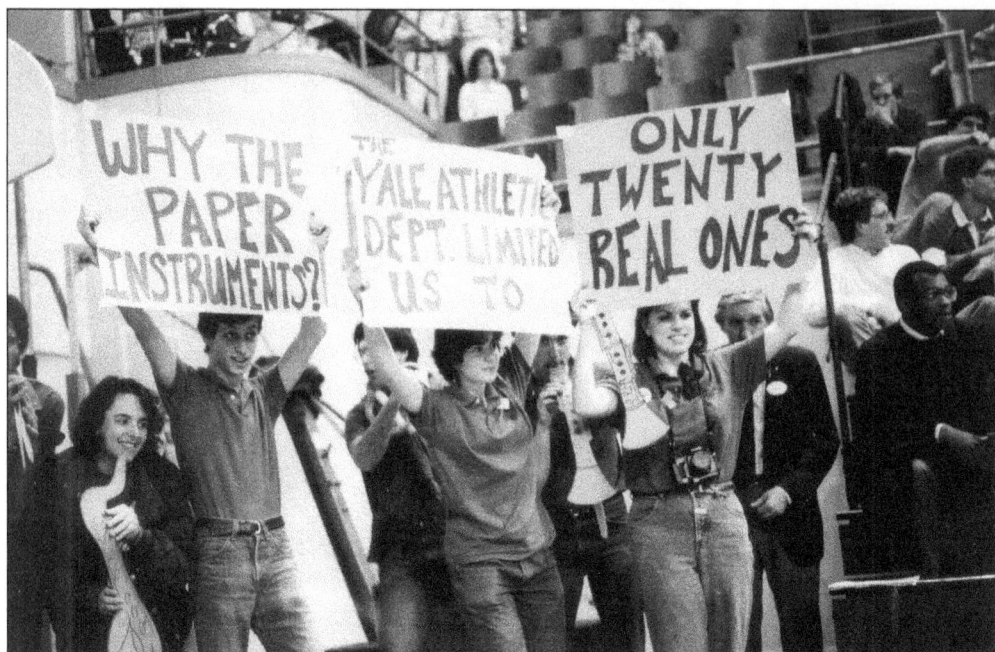

NO HOST BAND, 1987. At the same 1987 contest where the number of band members had been limited to 20, the Yale University band was strangely missing. It had been replaced at its own home games by a professional Dixieland group. In the above picture, Penn Band members wave signs poking fun at this odd circumstance.

Six

THE PROGRESSIVE BAND

Today the University of Pennsylvania's student body is a model for diversity. But this was not always the case. Similar to other institutions across the United States, women and African Americans struggled for equal opportunities at the University of Pennsylvania for decades. These struggles were mirrored in performing arts and athletics on the Penn campus.

Marching bands are sociological phenomena much like military organizations and athletics teams. Differences in economic background, gender, race, and religion are transcended by members working together towards a common goal. From its beginnings, the Penn Band was a group that challenged these social barriers on the Penn campus. In 1897, one of the original members of the inaugural band was an African American. Pictured at the top of the image on page 12 is the first African American member of the group, holding a flag. His name was Ben, and he was said to be a janitor at the Delta Phi fraternity house. In 1958, under the direction of Bruce Montgomery, the band was conducted by an African American student named James DePreist on Franklin Field for the very first time.

For decades, the Penn Band was an all-male organization, and women were not allowed on Franklin Field—it was believed to be bad luck. In 1962, Louise Erlich became the first female band member to perform in the concert band. By 1968, nine women were members of the group. Despite changes seen at other universities nationwide, even female cheerleaders did not appear on the field until the late 1960s. In 1969, Lynn Leopold became the first female band member to step on Franklin Field. Shortly afterwards, women were allowed in the group, and the group's first female president and vice president (Peggy Schnarr and Lynn Leopold) were elected in 1972. Today women constitute over half the membership of the organization.

STEREOTYPES. At left, a 1905 F. Earl Christy postcard image depicted a female Quaker fan with drum in hand. Until the fall of 1969, women were not allowed on Franklin Field, despite changes elsewhere across the country. Below is an image of a cheerleading squad at Franklin Field, around 1923. Both the Penn Band and the cheerleaders were all-male organizations until well into the late 1960s. (Left, collections of the University of Pennsylvania Archives; below, *The Record*, 1955.)

THE ALL-MALE TRADITION. Seen here are four unidentified members of the Penn Band from the 1960s. Despite its progressiveness, the Penn Band remained a solely male tradition, embracing female members much later than other collegiate organizations. In the 1940s, the Pennsylvania State University Marching Band became one of the first schools on record to have females in their ranks performing on the football field.

JAMES DEPREIST, 1957. Shown here is James DePreist, president of the Penn Band in 1957, conducting the Penn Band at Franklin Field. DePreist earned his bachelor's and master's degrees from the university and became a world-renowned conductor, holding such positions as music director of the Oregon Symphony Orchestra and faculty member of the Julliard School of Music. In 1976, he received an honorary degree from the University of Pennsylvania in recognition of his achievements. (*The Record*, 1957.)

THE PERCUSSIONISTS OF THE PENN BAND, 1960s. Pictured here is the percussion line of the Penn Band. Director Joseph A. Colontanio is seen to the far right. On the far left is one of the first African American band members to be photographed since James DePreist's tunure as president of the band.

LOUISE ERLICH, 1962. Above, Louise Erlich, (shown playing her clarinet) holds the distinction of being the first female member of the organization. While she could not march on Franklin Field, she served as a music librarian and as a member of the symphonic band. This opened the door for a number of other female instrumentalists to join the organization. By 1968, the symphonic band had nine females in its ranks, as seen below. (Above, collections of the University of Pennsylvania).

THE GENTLEMEN PERFORMING FOR THE LADIES AT HILL HOUSE, 1960s. By 1940, women comprised approximately 30 percent of the student body at the university. However, it was not until 1960 that a dorm was constructed specifically for women: Hill House, located at Thirty-fourth and Walnut Streets. Seen here is the all-male Penn Band visiting and performing for the female residents of the dorm. The now coed Penn Band still performs on football game days at the now coed Hill House. (Photographs by John Keplinger.)

NEW YORK WORLD'S FAIR 1964·1965 CORPORATION

Daily Pass

GOOD FOR ONE ADMISSION ON DATE STAMPED BELOW

UNISPHERE
presented by (USS)
United States
Steel

©1961, 1962
New York
World's Fair
1964-1965
Corporation

OPENING DAY
APRIL 22, 1964

The privileges
extended to the
holder of this
Pass shall at
all times be
subject to
the rules and
regulations of
the New York
World's Fair
1964—1965
Corporation

NOT TRANSFERABLE – VALID AT PASS GATES ONLY

22801

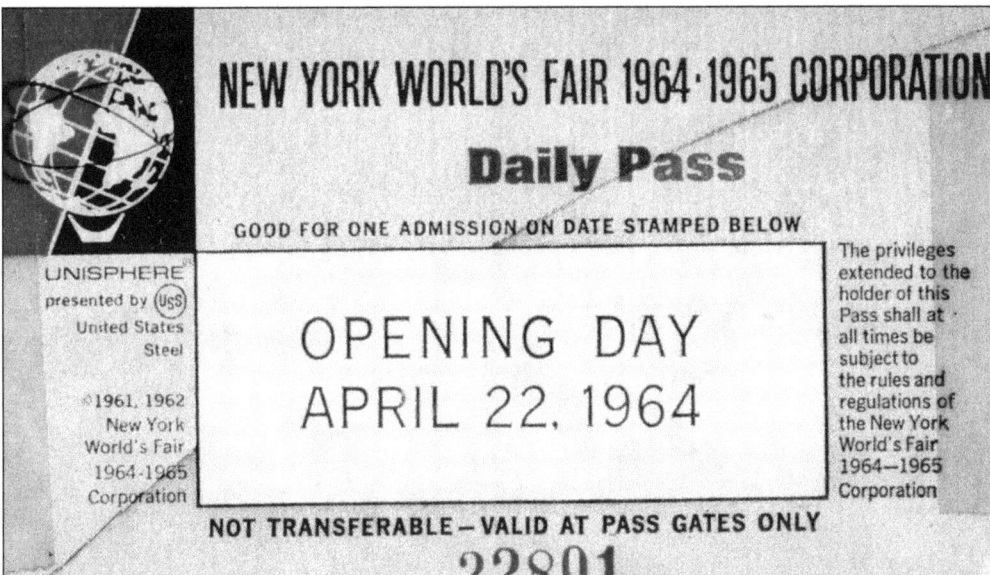

THE 1964 WORLD'S FAIR.
The performance at the
1964 New York World's Fair
also marked one of the first
recorded occasions that
females performed with
the traditionally all-male
organization at an outdoor
performance. Above is an
admission ticket from the
opening-day festivities. Below,
a member of the Penn Band is
seen socializing with some of
the female performers before
the event.

THE QUAKERETTES AT THE 1964 WORLD'S FAIR. **Above,** the New York World's Fair event also marked the premiere of the Quakerettes, a female cheering squad. The women that comprised the Quakerettes are, from left to right, the following: (first row) Susan Brumbaugh (class of 1965), Joann Roberts (captain, class of 1967), and Barbara Silver (class of 1967); (second row) Carol Jacobson (class of 1966), Barbara Meyers (class of 1967), Reid Stevens (class of 1967), Sharon Mandell (class of 1967), and Susan Scranton (class of 1967). Below, the Quakerettes are in a parade at the New York World's Fair.

DURING THE OUTDOOR CONCERT AT THE WORLD'S FAIR, 1964.
Above, a majorette performs a routine while the Penn Band plays. At right, one of the Quakerettes enjoys a dance with the Quaker mascot during the concert.

THE FIRST FEMALE CHEERLEADERS, 1968. Despite changes nationwide and active debate on campus, females had yet to find their way into the cheerleading squad (as well as the marching band) for most of the 1960s. That barrier was finally broken by the end of the decade with the first female cheerleaders. Following suit in 1969, Lynn Leopold became the first female band member to walk on Franklin Field, ending the all-male tradition of the marching band. Pictured here are the first female cheerleaders. They are, listed from left to right, (first row) Hary Sitgraves; (second row) Trish Tunstall and Fran Fiala; (third row) Adele Slatko, Sue Holmes, and Amanda Bird.

PEP RALLY PARADE BLOCK WITH CHEERLEADERS, 1968. This picture was taken before a pep rally in the fall of 1968. Pictured from left to right are the following: (first row) unidentified, Reina Marin, unidentified, Sherry Parker, and unidentified; (second row) Don Allen, unidentified, Laurie Dinardi, unidentified, Robert Hughes, Thomas Hall, Mike Hurwitz (drum major), and John White (conductor); (third row) Howard Ellis, Larry Gross, Timothy Campbell, Rob Rosenburg, Ken Gerstein, and unidentified; (fourth row) Robert S. Goodwin, Lance White, Frank Manola, George Enternmann, and two unidentified.

THE COED BAND, AROUND 1970. By the middle of the 1970s, females were fully integrated into the fabric of the organization, comprising a significant proportion of the group. The older gentleman standing to the right of the bass drum is Charles Barris, a graduate student who performed with the group and arranged music for the organization (including *The Gong Show* theme song).

EVOLUTION OF THE UNIFORM, 1970S. Most likely due to the increase in the number of females in the organization and change in the times, the nature of the uniform changed. As seen in both images, the collared shirt and black tie that was trademark of the 1960s was replaced by a more contemporary white-collar neck shirt.

IN THE STANDS OF FRANKLIN FIELD, 1970S. This is one of the first images of the newly coed band in the stands of Franklin Field. The integration of females in the organization also brought a distinct change in the instruments the organization played. Seen in pictures such as these are more woodwind and bells players than in decades past. Pictured with his back turned to the camera, conducting the band, is director Claude White.

MARIANNE ALVES, 1991. Pictured here is Marianne Alves (class of 1992), a tubist, who became the first female drum major in the Penn Band's 91-year history. Here she stands at Franklin Field, days after her selection as drum major. Since Alves's tenure, many other women have also filled the role. The first assistant female drum major was Ann McCarthy during the 1979–1980 season.

JAMES STALLWORTH AND R. GREER CHEESEMAN III, 1994. Pictured here is drum major James Stallworth (class of 1995, left) with director R. Greer Cheeseman III (class of 1977, right). Both are seen at a 1994 football game at Harvard University. Stallworth was only the second African American drum major in the organization's history; the first was Terrence Pinder (class of 1975).

Seven

THE HUGE,
THE ENORMOUS . . .

The 1970s brought further changes for the Penn Band. Simultaneous with the move to the Annenberg Center as the new home for the organization on the Penn campus, oversight of the band was transferred to the athletic department, although the Penn Band still maintains strong ties to the general undergraduate body.

In the early part of the 1970s, membership struggled. The times were marked by social unrest, and there was little interest in student activities on campus and a greater interest in political issues. At one point, membership dropped to under 50 members. In 1974 and 1979, respectively, the jazz band and the symphonic band became autonomous organizations outside of the auspices of the program.

All the while, the Penn Band continued its gradual transformation into the scramble band it would become for the remainder of the 20th century. In a tradition that developed across the Ivy League, the group became more irreverent with its comedic halftime. This form of entertainment raised eyebrows among administrators, as alumni complained about racy halftime shows. There were even discussions about disbanding and reorganizing the group.

The band ultimately prevailed under the baton of director Claude White, strong student leadership, and the help of administrators on the newly formed Band Policy Committee. In 1979, new uniforms replaced the familiar red blazer of the 1960s and included blue varsity sweaters and white pants. During the 1980s, the group continued its tradition of being the university's first ambassador, playing at events attended by dignitaries such as Pres. Ronald Reagan, Polish labor leader Lech Walesa, Chief Justice William Brenner, and novelist James Michener. The group sent representatives to Disney's Epcot Center All-Star Band to commemorate the opening of the park, and once again the group performed at the Miss America Pageant parade.

During the 1980s, band membership ballooned to over 300 members, the largest in the program's history, and the group's identity as a scramble band was firmly established. The Penn Band's introductory vaudeville-esque moniker at the beginning of each field show best embodies the spirit of the group as a fun-loving organization. The Penn Band is, "The Huge, the Enormous, the Well-Endowed, Undefeated, Ivy-League Champion, University of Pennsylvania Oxymoronic Fighting Quaker Marching Band!"

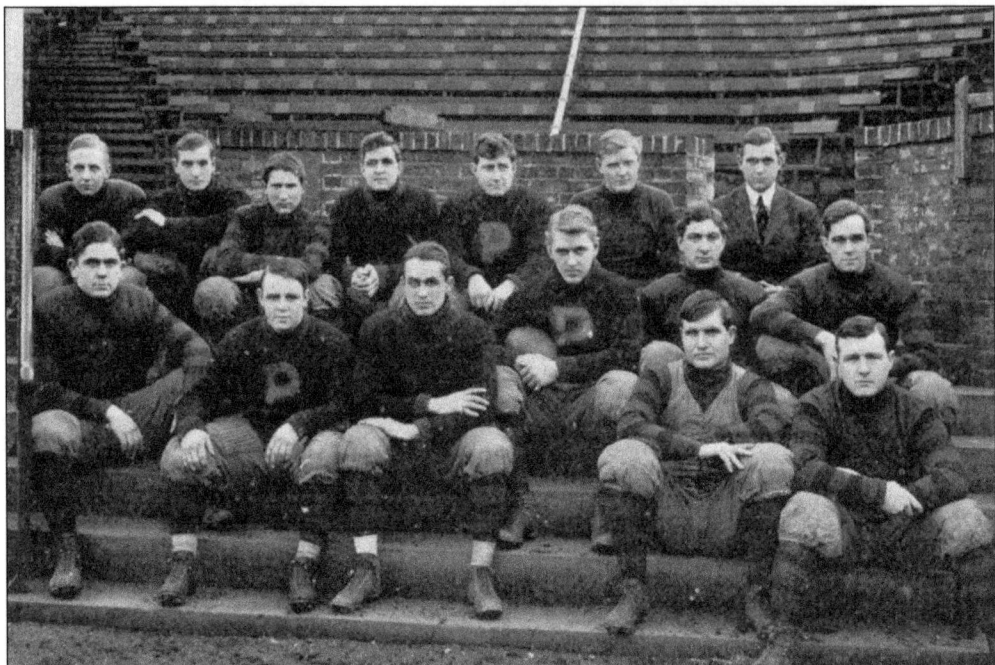

NEW UNIFORMS, 1979.
Pictured above is the 1901 varsity football team. The new uniforms introduced in the fall of 1979 were intended to mimic the varsity sweater uniform of previous university athletic teams. Unwittingly the Penn Band had emulated the uniform of the freshman band that had been formed at Penn in the 1930s. Below, baritone player Robert Polsky is seen here in the new uniform in 1979 on Franklin Field. (Above, *University of Pennsylvania Illustrated*.)

THE 1981 PENN BAND. The Penn Band sits in the stands during a game in 1981 at Franklin Field. Relative to the previous decade, the group shows evidence of tremendous growth in membership.

CLARINETISTS AT FRANKLIN FIELD, AROUND 1982. Shown here are two unidentified members of the band in the stands: one plays his clarinet while the other waves a pom-pom.

THE TRUMPET SECTION, AROUND 1983. The Penn Band's trumpet section performs in this photograph.

CLAUDE WHITE. Claude White is pictured here conducting the organization in rehearsal. White directed the University of Pennsylvania Band from 1973 to 1975 and from 1978 to 1994. During his tenure, White also served as director of the University Orchestra and Wind Ensemble.

PERCUSSIONISTS, AROUND 1983. Above, a cymbal player plays his part during a performance on the field. Below, Brad Lebo (class of 1983) prepares to cadence in front of the Annenberg Center; seen over his shoulder on the left is Doris Mack (class of 1977) in the background, a former president of the organization.

THE SOCIAL ORGANIZATION, AROUND 1983. In the 1970s and 1980s, the Penn Band focused more on the social aspects of the organization. Not only was the band service-oriented, but it also became a social outlet for the students, a role that it plays to this day. Above, students watch the game as a balloon floats overhead. Scott Lorimer (class of 1984) is seen standing to the far right; the identities of the other individuals are unknown. Below, three members pose for a portrait while in the stands at Franklin Field. The individual in the center is Larry Creswell (class of 1984); the identities of the other two individuals are unknown.

TUBA PLAYER WALKING ACROSS THE BRIDGE, AROUND 1981. Former band president Jeff Indrisano (class of 1982) is seen walking his tuba across the Locust Walk bridge on campus.

CLEARING SKIES AT FRANKLIN FIELD, AROUND 1983. Seen here are members of the Penn Band performing on the field at homecoming.

SPRINGTIME ON CAMPUS, EARLY 1990S. The Penn Band is pictured here walking across campus on a spring day. Unlike the previous generations of the group, the Penn Band now uses an alternative uniform after the conclusion of the football season.

LONG LINES, AROUND 1986. Above, the Penn Band forms a tunnel as a prelude to the entrance of the football team. Below, the group begins its entrance for its pregame performance. This entrance is one of the few times the group will actually march in a military style during its regular performance. Making these practices all the more remarkable is the number of members: during the mid-1980s, the group's membership surged to over 300, the largest in its history.

Policy Statement
Unanimously Adopted
Philadelphia, April 17, 1982

We, the leaders of the Ivy League Marching Bands, recognize the importance of our organizations for school spirit, and alumni and public relations. We feel that both cooperation with and support from our school administrations are vital to the production of quality entertainment at intercollegiate sporting events. Recognizing and encouraging the diversity of our organizations, we believe we have a valid place within the framework of Ivy League Athletics. We acknowledge past concerns, and accept responsibility for the role we play in the educational processes at our respective institutions.

A spirit of cooperation among our bands has been established and will continue.

THE IVY BANDS CONFERENCE, 1982. The satirical halftime shows of the Ivy-League bands were at the center of controversy that became subject matter for national publications such as the *Wall Street Journal*, *Sports Illustrated*, and the *New York Times*. In response to the need for more proactive communication among the bands, the Penn Band started the Ivy Bands Conference in April 1982. As a result of the first meeting, a policy statement (shown here) was ratified by all eight Ivy bands and published, and the student-leader meeting has been held annually ever since.

ALUMNI DAY, LATE 1980S. Shown here is the Penn Band leading the Alumni Day procession across the Locust Walk bridge on campus. In contrast to its participation in the event earlier in the century, the band has a more casual appearance in uniform, with members (seen in striped polo shirts) wearing shorts and sneakers. Leading the parade is drum major Ron Shelkin (class of 1989).

FOUNDED 1787

The College of Physicians of Philadelphia

Celebrates Its

200th Anniversary

A Bicentennial Address

by

Ronald Wilson Reagan

President of The United States

PRES. RONALD REAGAN, 1987. Members of the Penn Band had the opportunity to perform for President Reagan at the Franklin Plaza Hotel in Center City, Philadelphia, in March 1987. The president's speech was part of an event celebrating the 200th anniversary of the College of Physicians of Philadelphia. Shown here is the cover of the program for the event.

Instrumentalists
See the world.

Come out and be a part of the rowdiest, wittiest, most fun to be with Band in the Ivy League. Travel to exotic places like New Hampshire and New Jersey.

The Penn Band

It's not just an adventure. It's a hell of a lot of fun.

INTRO MEETING: Sept. 5 6:00 PM 511 Annenberg Center For more info - call 898-8719

See us at Performing Arts night.

INTRODUCTORY MEETING ADVERTISEMENT, 1986. This advertisement appeared in the student newspaper in September 1986, advertising the group's introductory meeting for new members.

THE NEW DRUM MAJOR. In stark contrast to the drum majors of the early half of the century—whose primary role was the marching direction and baton twirling—the drum majors of the 1970s and onwards took on a different look and function. These drum majors served as the primary conductors of the organization, distinguished not by their military decorum and precision, but by their charisma, showmanship, and musicianship. Shown above is 1985–1986 drum major Chip Bayers (class of 1986); shown below is Ron Shelkin (class of 1989), the drum major conducting the Penn Band during a halftime show.

THE TUBA SECTION, 1986. Coinciding with the dramatic growth of the organization during the 1980s was the growth of the tuba section. To complement halftime show themes, every week the tubists would use their sousaphone bells to spell out entire words and phrases. Here they are seen spelling out "SPACE4RENT."

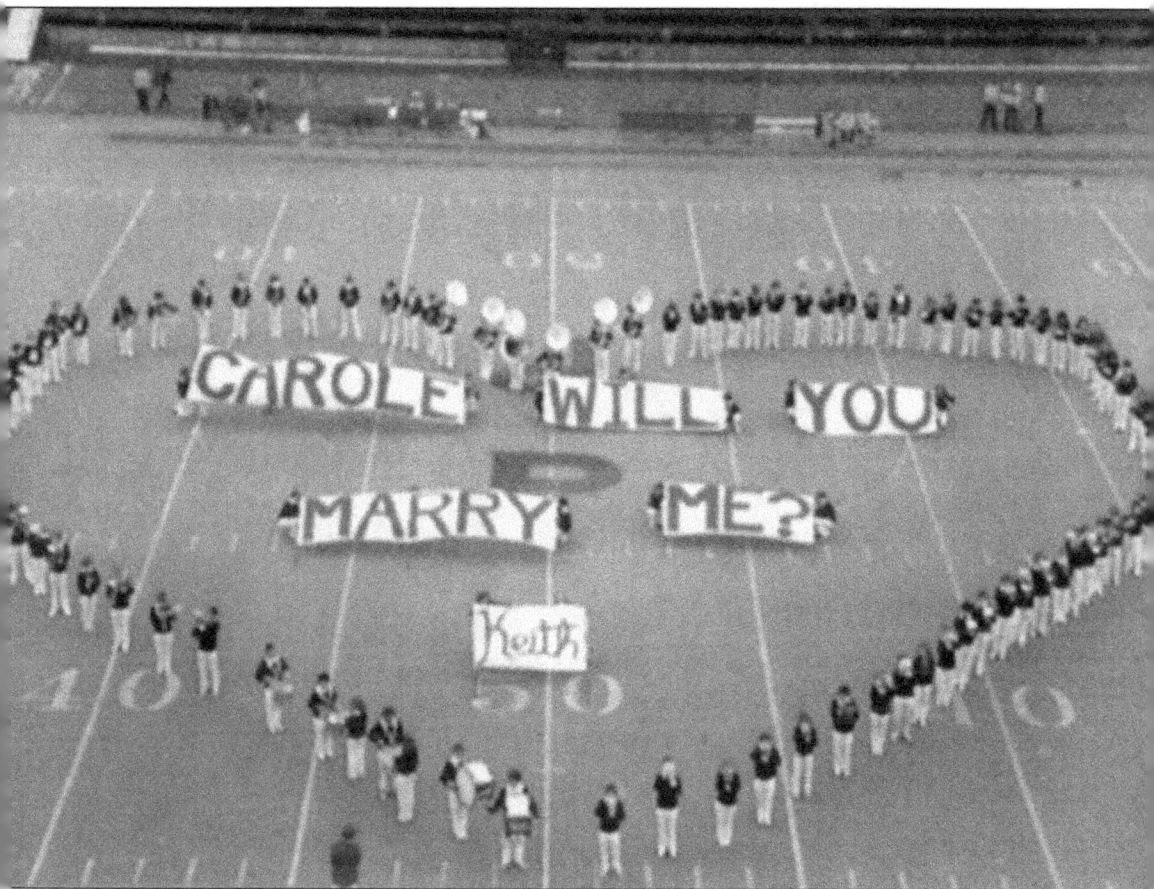

THE WEDDING PROPOSAL, 1986. In 1986, Keith P. Fungerman (class of 1981) resorted to an unusual method of proposing to his love, Carole Bergman. At the University of Pennsylvania–Lafayette University football game at Franklin Field, the Penn Band helped relay his marriage proposal via a special halftime show. Fortunately for him, Bergman accepted.

CHEER, PENNSYLVANIA!, 1983. The arrival of this album, the first in 20 years for the organization, was met with much anticipation among the Penn community. The album was recorded outdoors at Franklin Field.

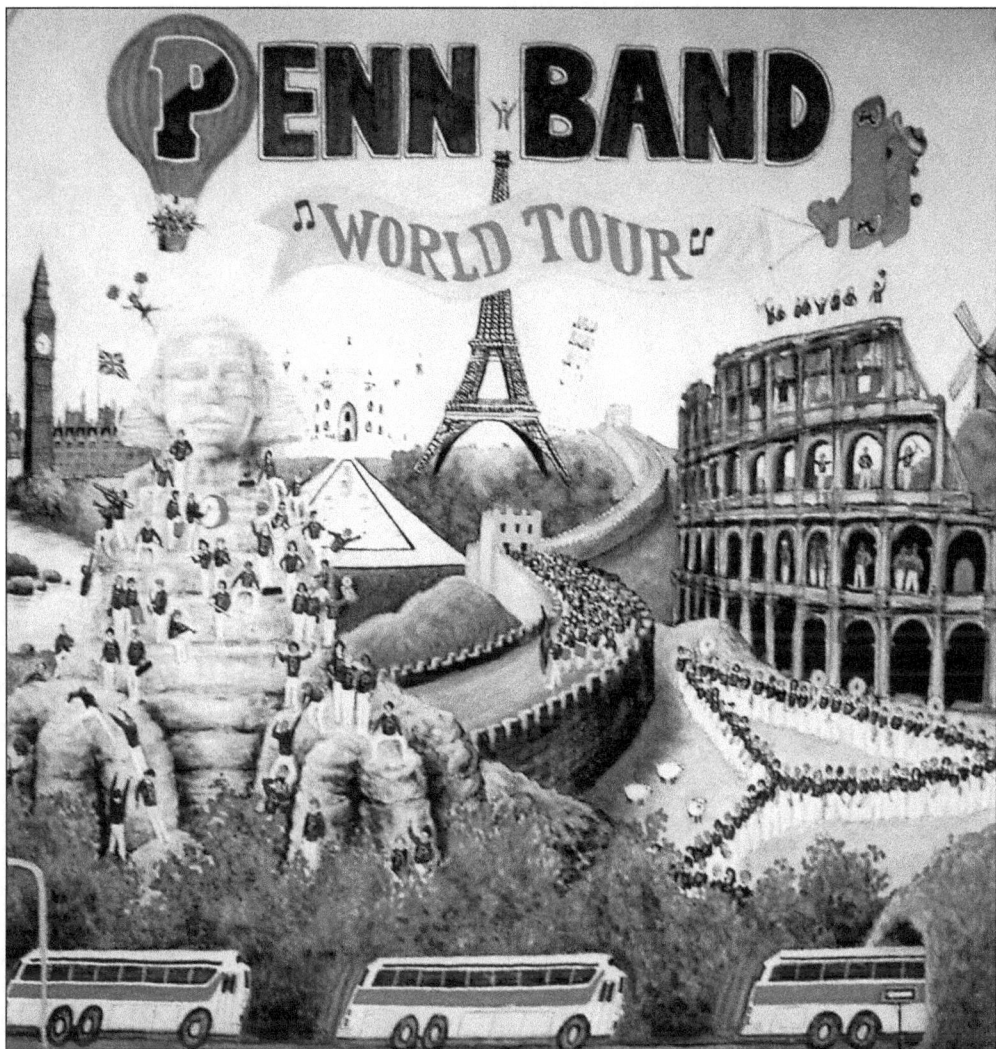

PENN BAND: WORLD TOUR, **1986.** This album's detailed cover art pays homage to the group's penchant for road trips. The album was recorded in the Palestra.

THE PEN BAND LIVE AT SMOKE'S, 1989. The Penn Band's third album of the 1980s featured Smokey Joe's, a pub that has been a long-time favorite destination amongst members of the student body. The album was recorded in the Palestra, and featured satirical voice tracks in addition to songs.

Samuel Lange Comes Home, Late 1980s. Samuel Lange (class of 1947) makes a return visit to Franklin Field, decades after his tenure as drum major of the Penn Band in the 1940s. During the Penn Band's halftime performance, he performed his trademark routine, including the ceremonial baton toss over the goalpost.

THE PENN BAND ON THE STEPS OF THE FISCHER FINE ARTS LIBRARY, 1993. Seen here is the Penn Band posing for a portrait on the steps of the library in 1993. This image ultimately became the cover art for the group's 1993 CD album *A Toast to Dear Old Penn*, its first CD production. The album included tracks from record albums dating back to 1926. The image pays tribute to the photograph of the band in its first year, as seen on page 12.

THE CENTENNIAL BAND, 1997. The group achieved centennial status in 1997, a distinction held by a small but growing number of university bands nationwide. The event was commemorated with much celebration, including a proclamation from the General Alumni Society, the recording of a CD (*5 Score and Several Years to Go*), the establishment of a centennial endowment fund, and a homecoming gala celebration in downtown Philadelphia.

THE BAND IN PERFORMANCE, 1995. The band is seen here performing its traditional pregame

performance at Franklin Field.

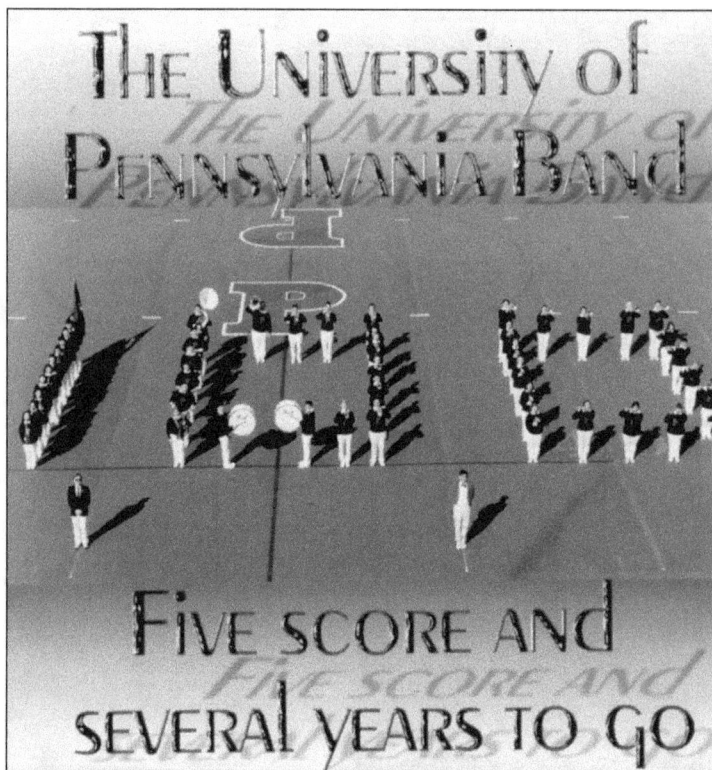

5 SCORE AND SEVERAL YEARS TO GO, 1997. In 1997, the Penn Band released its second CD recording (cover shown here) to celebrate its centennial anniversary. The album not only included recordings of several of the school songs, but also a vast repertoire of contemporary marching band tunes interlaced with a satiric script not unlike those written for halftime shows.

R. GREER CHEESEMAN III AND WALTER GALLAGHER, 1996. This is a portrait of Walter Gallagher (left, class of 1937) and band director R. Greer Cheeseman III (right), taken at alumni day in 1996. During his time in the band, Gallagher was a percussionist. To this day, he still joins the band at alumni events to play his instrument, especially when the band performs *Men of Pennsylvania*.

WHEREAS, in 1897, the year Houston Hall sprung up as the first student union building stirrings, rumblings, and tootings of The Penn Band's impending existence appeared in The Daily Pennsylvanian;

WHEREAS, by 1898, twenty-seven instruments, including flutes, cornets, clarinets, trumpets, trombones, tubas, and saxophones with musicians attached were well established as the first such ensemble in The Ivy League;

WHEREAS, in the Roaring Twenties, John Philip Sousa thrice conducted The Penn Band, and declared the University of Pennsylvania Band March to be the best of marches, excepting only his own;

WHEREAS, in 1970, the Band drummed up enough faculty support to go completely co-ed, thus creating a richer, more harmonious sound;

WHEREAS, over the decades, The Penn Band has set the tone and the beat for student rallies, parades, and graduation exercises and has provided lively accompaniment, spirited inspiration, and comic relief to the Quakers in all their endeavors on Franklin Field, at the Palestra, and on fields and courts far from home;

WHEREAS, The Penn Band is self-supporting, playing professional engagements to raise money for stylish uniforms, but always putting most of their money where their music is, in their reeds, their percussion, and their brass;

WHEREAS, The Penn Band, has played for many well-known people and occasions, and was the first college band to appear in the Macy's Thanksgiving Day Parade;

WHEREAS, The Penn Band, now 144 musicians strong and the largest band in the Ivy League with the most diverse repertoire, keeps alive the tradition of University songs in all their verve and variety for generations of students and alumni;

WHEREAS, loyal alumni come back on Homecoming and Alumni Day and join in as if they have never left — playing once more and always with feeling;

THEREFORE, be it resolved that the Awards and Resolution Committee of the General Alumni Society, does hereby proudly and gratefully commend The Penn Band, acknowledging it as "the undefeated champions of The Ivy League," on the occasion of its first 100 years, and in anticipation of many rousing years to come.

MARTHA Z. STACHITAS, CW'75
Executive Secretary, General Alumni Society

ELSIE STERLING HOWARD, CW'68
President, General Alumni Society

NOVEMBER 7, 1997

RECOGNITION FROM THE GENERAL ALUMNI SOCIETY, 1997. The General Alumni Society of the University of Pennsylvania recognized the Penn Band's centennial anniversary and long history of achievement with a proclamation, shown here.

REFERENCES

University of Pennsylvania. *The Record*. Philadelphia: University of Pennsylvania Press, 1895.

University of Pennsylvania. *The Record*. Philadelphia: University of Pennsylvania Press, 1919.

University of Pennsylvania. *The Record*. Philadelphia: University of Pennsylvania Press, 1939.

University of Pennsylvania. *The Record*. Philadelphia: University of Pennsylvania Press, 1955.

University of Pennsylvania. *The Record*. Philadelphia: University of Pennsylvania Press, 1957.

Clarke, H. A. *Songs of the University of Pennsylvania*. Philadelphia: University of Pennsylvania Glee Club, 1879.

Miller, William Otto. *Songs of the University of Pennsylvania*. New York: Hinds and Noble, 1909.

Nitzsche, George. *University of Pennsylvania Illustrated*. Philadelphia: John C. Winston Company, 1901.

Range II, Thomas E., and Sean Patrick Smith. *The Penn State Blue Band: A Century of Pride and Precision*. University Park, PA: Pennsylvania State University Press, 1999.

Rottenberg, Daniel. *Fight On, Pennsylvania: A Century of Red and Blue Football*. Philadelphia: Trustees of the University of Pennsylvania, 1985.

University of Pennsylvania Archives

University of Pennsylvania Band Archives

INDEX

Visit us at
arcadiapublishing.com

www.ingramcontent.com/pod-product-compliance
Lightning Source LLC
Chambersburg PA
CBHW050605110426
42813CB00008B/2466